"In true Tara-Leigh fashion, this study is easy to follow while also challenging you to dig deeper into what the Word is saying. It's more than simply reading the Bible and answering some questions. It's a test to gauge your spiritual walk, to ask the hard questions, and to be challenged with each turn of the page about what the Holy Spirit is revealing. Whether you are a new believer or well-versed in theological teachings, this study has something to offer everyone."

Clare Thompson Sims, D-Group member

"This study delivers what D-Group has been doing for years. Instead of feeding the readers answers, it empowers them to do the work of arriving at answers through the careful study and close reading of God's Word, allowing them to take ownership of their continued growth and faith in King Jesus. What a thrilling start of a memorable new series!"

Zuzana Johansen, D-Group member

"This study helps the reader connect the Old Testament with the New by giving the perspective of the Jewish culture and customs during Jesus's day. This lens provides clarity as to why Jesus ministered and spoke as He did while interacting with both Jews and Gentiles. It also clearly communicates the relevance and life-changing power of Jesus's teachings for Christians today. It's a road map, pulling from the pages of the Old Testament and connecting it to the Gospels, pointing to our victory in Christ on the cross."

Jeremy Hall, D-Group member

"*Knowing Jesus as King* combines a deep dive into the book of Matthew with the structure of D-Group. Having been in D-Group from the very start—fifteen years ago—I can confidently say the structure creates the consistency it demands and bears much fruit for any believer. Buckle up and have faith that God will reveal Himself to you as the promised and present King over the next ten weeks."

Meghann Glenn, D-Group charter member

KNOWING
JESUS
AS KING

Also by Tara-Leigh Cobble

The Bible Recap:
A One-Year Guide to Reading and Understanding the Entire Bible

The Bible Recap Study Guide:
Daily Questions to Deepen Your Understanding of the Entire Bible

The Bible Recap Journal:
Your Daily Companion to the Entire Bible

The Bible Recap Discussion Guide:
Weekly Questions for Group Conversation on the Entire Bible

The Bible Recap Kids' Devotional:
365 Reflections and Activities for Children and Families

The God Shot:
100 Snapshots of God's Character in Scripture

Israel:
Beauty, Light, and Luxury

THE BIBLE RECAP KNOWING JESUS SERIES

KNOWING JESUS AS KING

A 10-SESSION STUDY ON THE GOSPEL OF MATTHEW

TARA-LEIGH COBBLE,
GENERAL EDITOR

WRITTEN BY THE D-GROUP THEOLOGY & CURRICULUM TEAM

BETHANYHOUSE
a division of Baker Publishing Group
Minneapolis, Minnesota

© 2024 by Tara-Leigh Cobble

Published by Bethany House Publishers
Minneapolis, Minnesota
BethanyHouse.com

Bethany House Publishers is a division of
Baker Publishing Group, Grand Rapids, Michigan

Printed in the United States of America

ISBN 9780764243561 (paper)
ISBN 9781493446872 (ebook)

Library of Congress Cataloging-in-Publication Control Number: 2023050022

Unless otherwise indicated, Scripture quotations are from The Holy Bible, English Standard Version® (ESV®), copyright © 2001 by Crossway, a publishing ministry of Good News Publishers. Used by permission. All rights reserved. ESV Text Edition: 2016

Scripture quotations identified KJV are from the King James Version of the Bible.

Scripture quotations identified NIV are taken from the Holy Bible, New International Version®, NIV®. Copyright © 1973, 1978, 1984, 2011 by Biblica, Inc.® Used by permission of Zondervan. All rights reserved worldwide. www .zondervan.com. The "NIV" and "New International Version" are trademarks registered in the United States Patent and Trademark Office by Biblica, Inc.®

The D-Group Theology & Curriculum Team is Laura Buchelt, Emily Pickell, Meg Mitchell, Evaline Asmah, and Tara-Leigh Cobble.

The general editor is represented by Alive Literary Agency, www.AliveLiterary.com.

Interior design by Nadine Rewa.
Cover design by Dan Pitts
Author image from © Meshali Mitchell

Baker Publishing Group publications use paper produced from sustainable forestry practices and postconsumer waste whenever possible.

24 25 26 27 28 29 30   7 6 5 4 3 2 1

This book is dedicated to the original members of D-Group, who signed up to pursue God and study His Word together, long before any of us knew what great joy He had in store: Meghann Glenn, Holly Shanahan, Meredith Tatum, Kate Gaffney, Heather Siders, Cory Cooper, Elizabeth Sullivan, Kara Villines, Laura Bouknight, Caroline McClure.

CONTENTS

INTRODUCTION

The Gospels (Matthew, Mark, Luke, and John) offer us a fourfold telling of Jesus's story. Some may wonder why this is necessary, but the fascinating truth is that each gospel speaks to a specific audience and emphasizes a unique aspect of who Jesus is. Additionally, the areas where they overlap verify the authenticity of the full narrative.

Matthew writes about King Jesus—His authority, His royalty, and His throne that will last forever. Mark writes about Jesus as the Suffering Servant, the One whose suffering would eternally serve all who call on His name. Luke, drawing on Jesus's humanity, emphasizes Jesus as Savior of mankind, which seems fitting since Luke was a doctor. And John, the self-proclaimed favorite of our Lord, repeatedly highlights that Jesus is God. These four narratives help us see Jesus from various angles, capturing different facets of His glory—King, Servant, Savior/Man, God. These characteristics may seem opposed to each other, but they actually present us with a fuller understanding of who He is. All four accounts are not only necessary but beautiful!

The text of Matthew doesn't identify its author, but the early church fathers seemed to agree that Matthew, the disciple of Jesus, wrote this book. Matthew, who also went by the name Levi, was a Jew who likely lived and worked near Capernaum along the Sea of Galilee. Until Jesus called him to be a disciple (Matthew 9:9–13), he was a tax collector. It's hard for us to grasp how audacious it was for Jesus to choose a tax collector as one of His disciples. This was scandalous! Matthew, a Jewish man, worked for the Roman army—the oppressive enemy of his people. He collected taxes for Rome's brutal empire, funding the very army that would threaten, torture, and kill other Jews. As if that weren't enough, first-century tax collectors were notorious for being corrupt, taking above and beyond the required Roman tax to line their own pockets.

Matthew's transformation from his identity as a Jewish tax collector for Rome to a disciple of Jesus was a dramatic one, establishing him as the perfect person to record an eyewitness account of the life of Christ. And because he had to be meticulous with money, there's no doubt that he was meticulous with the details of his gospel.

Matthew seems to have written primarily to help Greek-speaking Jews see that Jesus was the King they'd been looking for. We get a few hints that his audience was Jewish: He quoted the Old Testament sixty-two times—more than any other gospel writer—he didn't explain the Jewish cultural norms like John and Mark did, he regularly used the phrase *kingdom of heaven* (a reverential Jewish expression), and he began his account with the genealogy of Jesus, something a non-Jew would have cared little about.

If you were a first-century Jewish person who believed God would eventually send a new King, would Matthew's account of Jesus's life cause you to see the truth that Jesus was and is that King? Let's find out together!

HOW TO USE THIS STUDY

While Bible study is vital to the Chrisitan walk, a well-rounded spiritual life comes from engaging with other spiritual disciplines as well. This study is designed not only to equip you with greater knowledge and theological depth, but to help you engage in other formative practices that will create a fuller, more fulfilling relationship with Jesus. We want to see you thrive in every area of your life with God!

Content and Questions

In each of the ten weeks of this study, the teaching and questions are divided into six days, but feel free to do it all at once if that's more manageable for your schedule. If you choose to complete each week's study in one sitting, keep in mind that there are still aspects you will want to be mindful of each day: the daily Bible reading, Scripture memorization, and the weekly challenge. These are best attended to throughout the week.

Daily Bible Reading

The daily Bible reading corresponds to our study. It will take an average of three minutes per day to simply read (not study) the text. If you're an auditory learner, you may prefer to listen to an audio version of these Bible chapters.

Even if you decide to go through the week's content and questions in one sitting, we still encourage you to make the daily Bible reading a part of your regular daily rhythm. Establishing a habit of reading the Word every day will help fortify your faith and create greater connections with God.

If you decide to break the study up into the six allotted days each week, your daily Bible reading will align with your study. Days 1–5 will follow our study of Matthew, Day 6 features a psalm that corresponds to our reading, and Day 7 serves as a catch-up day in case you fall behind.

Scripture Memorization

Memorizing Scripture isn't busy work! It's an important part of hiding God's Word in our hearts (Psalm 119:11). Our passage—Matthew 6:25–34—is a powerful truth about valuing eternal things above all else. We encourage you to practice it cumulatively—that is, *add* to what you're practicing each week instead of *replacing* it. We quote the English Standard Version (and some of our resources are in that translation as well), but feel free to memorize it in whatever translation you prefer. We suggest working on each week's verse(s) throughout the week, not just at the last minute. We've provided some free tools to help you with this, including a weekly verse song: MyDGroup.org/Resources/Matthew.

Weekly Challenge

This is our practical response to what we've learned each week. We want to be "doers of the word, and not hearers only" (James 1:22). You'll find a variety of challenges, and we encourage you to lean into them all—especially the ones you find *most* challenging! This will help strengthen your spiritual muscles and encourage you in your faith. As with the memory verse, you'll want to begin this practice earlier in the week, especially because some weekly challenges include things to do each day of the week (e.g., prayers, journaling, etc.).

Resources

This is a Scripture-heavy study, and you'll find yourself looking up passages often. If you're new to studying Scripture, this will be a great way to dig in and sharpen your skills! You will feel more equipped and less intimidated as you move through each chapter. Some questions may ask you to refer to a Bible dictionary, commentary, or Greek or Hebrew lexicon, but you don't need to purchase those tools. There are lots of free options available online. We've linked to some of our favorite tools—plus additional resources like podcasts, articles, and apps—at MyDGroup.org/Resources/Matthew.

Matthew 1–4:
Origin of the King

Note: If you haven't yet read "How to Use This Study" on page 13, please do that before continuing. It will provide you with a proper framework and helpful tools.

Scripture to Memorize

Therefore I tell you, do not be anxious about your life, what you will eat or what you will drink, nor about your body, what you will put on. Is not life more than food, and the body more than clothing?

Matthew 6:25

DAILY BIBLE READING

Day 1: Matthew 1

Day 2: Matthew 2

Day 3: Matthew 3

Day 4: Matthew 4:1–11

Day 5: Matthew 4:12–25

Day 6: Psalm 2

Day 7: Catch-Up Day

Corresponds to Days 275–278 of *The Bible Recap*.

WEEKLY CHALLENGE

See page 39 for more information.

Matthew 1

◣◢ READ MATTHEW 1

The New Testament isn't where we first see the concept of a King who would redeem and reign over all nations. The need for a King to rule goes all the way back to Genesis 3—when the first humans, made in the image of God, willingly gave away their kingship and dominion to the enemy, who was disguised as a manipulative serpent.

From that moment on, humanity felt its need for a King to reverse the curse of death and separation from God. But God wasn't willing to leave them to their own devices—He provided covenants throughout the Old Testament that pointed to His eventual redemption of humanity. God chose for Himself the unlikely nation of Israel, fathered by Abraham, as the origin point of His redemption plan (Genesis 12:1–3) and the lineage of the King (Matthew 2:2).

The Old Testament follows this unlikely nation as it stumbles its way forward with a hope and longing for a new King. We'll look back at several of those moments in this chapter.

Read 2 Samuel 7:12–16. Why is it significant that Jesus is the son of David?

Read Genesis 12:3. Why is it significant that Jesus is the son of Abraham?

Matthew's genealogy has a few interesting things to note: First, this genealogy follows the bloodline of Joseph—who isn't biologically related to Jesus but is His legal father. Second, this genealogy includes women and Gentiles (non-Jews), which was highly unusual for the time. Third, it's likely that Matthew skipped some generations along the way in order to get his trio of fourteen generations.

This isn't deception on Matthew's part—it's how genealogies were often written to make them easier to memorize. This particular genealogy also uses the sum of seven plus seven—seven being the number of completion or perfection—making the total fourteen to signify *double* completion or perfection. Essentially, through the numbers given in this lineage, Matthew was saying that Jesus is the culmination of this complete and perfect setup for the redemption of humanity as its eternal King!

What might Matthew be trying to communicate by including women and Gentiles? What does it mean for you personally?

Matthew's account of the birth of Jesus focuses specifically on Joseph's point of view.

Read Matthew 1:18–25. What does this reveal about the type of man Joseph was? Which characteristics of Joseph are convicting or encouraging to you?

In the angel's conversation with Joseph, another prophecy was fulfilled about the name of the coming King. Quoting Isaiah 7:14, the angel said the King would be born to a virgin, and His name would be Immanuel, which means "God with us." The word *Immanuel* reveals both the deity and the humanity of the coming King:

GOD with us—deity
God *WITH US*—humanity

Do a web search to find the meaning of the name Jesus. How does it correspond to the name Immanuel? What does it tell us about why He was born and what He would accomplish?

Read Philippians 2:5–11. What particular aspects of this passage correspond to the theme of Jesus as King?

Knowing the end of the story, what is your response to the person of Jesus?

Matthew 2

◢◣ READ MATTHEW 2

Hold loosely to your nativity sets, because today's study is about to shake some things up! Matthew 2:11 tells us that the wise men found the *child* (not baby) in the *house* (not where animals were fed). And while there were three gifts, there may not have been three wise men. The gifts were likely brought by a large group of wise men—like pooling your money with friends to buy a crib, instead of everyone buying separate, smaller gifts for a baby shower. So add a few dozen Magi (wise men) to your nativity set and move them to a different room in your home, because it likely took them between six months and two years to arrive.

The wise men from the east—possibly Gentiles or exiled Jews who knew the prophecies about the coming King—traveled a great distance hoping to find and worship Him. Their first stop in Jerusalem made sense because it was the center of Jewish life. However, they were met by a deceitful Roman governor and religious leaders who knew about the prophecy but seemed disinterested in worshiping the King themselves.

Using a Bible dictionary, look up the terms below and write out a few notes on what you find. You can also use the information in Matthew 2 to fill in the table below.

Magi	
Herod the Great	
Chief Priests	
Scribes	

The Magi, Herod, and the religious leaders had three unique responses to the birth of the King. How did they each respond? **Fill in the table below.**

	Response to Jesus's Birth
Magi	
Herod the Great	
Religious Leaders	

What does it reveal about God that He would draw the wise men from far away to come worship Jesus?

What gets in the way of your worshiping Him?

Matthew 2:10 says, "When they saw the star, they rejoiced exceedingly with great joy." The star that pointed the way to the King brought those who were seeking Him great joy (because He's where the joy is!). The same star that brought them joy and anticipation had a different impact on King Herod—it made the power-hungry ruler spiral into fear. And it did very little to penetrate the hardened hearts of the religious leaders; they may have followed the rules with precision, but they failed to demonstrate love for God and His people.

The second half of Matthew 2 chronicles three events that fulfill additional Old Testament prophecies. This reinforces the identity of King Jesus, even when He was just a child.

Review 2:13–15.

What was the situation and what action was taken?

Who did Joseph trust?

What was the significance of the prophecy (Hosea 11:1)?

Review 2:16–18.

What was the situation and what action was taken?

Who did Herod trust?

What was the significance of the prophecy (Jeremiah 31:15)?

Review 2:19–23.

What was the situation and what action was taken?

Who did Joseph trust?

What was the significance of the prophecy?

This section doesn't seem to refer to one specific Old Testament prophecy. Matthew used the phrase *spoken by the prophets*, which may indicate that it's not a direct quote but more of a summary of the prophetic expectation. The prophets said the King would be born into obscurity, humility, and rejection. Nazareth, a town with a seedy reputation, would've fit that definition perfectly.

What stood out to you in today's reading? Are there any action steps you need to take as a result?

Matthew 3

 READ MATTHEW 3

Today's reading jumps ahead about thirty years to where we're introduced to John the Baptist (we'll call him JTB to help distinguish him from John the gospel writer), and we see Jesus's ministry officially commissioned.

In the first century, logic would suggest you speak in a city if you wanted to draw a crowd. But JTB didn't seem to rely on conventional human wisdom. He did the opposite of what seemed obvious. From preaching in the wilderness of Judea (think Arizona desert with the occasional oasis), to wearing impractical clothes made of itchy camel hair, JTB wasn't motivated by the opinions of the masses but by the message he carried.

Look up Matthew 3:2–3 in a Bible commentary and jot down a few insights about the following words or phrases:

- Repent. _____
  _____

- The kingdom of heaven is at hand. _____
  _____

- Prepare the way of the Lord; make His paths straight. _____
  _____

From the desert wilderness, JTB preached repentance and invited those who confessed and repented to be baptized. Interestingly, his message of hope turned a bit cold when the Pharisees and Sadducees arrived from

Jerusalem—a four-day round trip—to investigate JTB and his actions (John 1:19–28).

In a Bible dictionary, look up Pharisees and Sadducees. Which characteristics of these two religious groups would JTB likely have been displeased with?

JTB knew they weren't really looking for the Messiah King. Their lives showed no evidence of the changed heart that accompanies true repentance. He even boldly stated that their status as children of Abraham didn't grant them entry into the kingdom—and in fact, they were teetering toward destruction. Then he humbly pointed to the King, the hope of the Holy Spirit, and the reality of eternal judgment.

There are modern parallels here that are too important to pass up. Today, there are men and women who call themselves Christians who genuinely believe that being in church every week and not doing too many "bad things" qualifies them as genuine followers of Jesus. This passage reveals the flaw in that logic. Salvation comes only by recognizing and confessing your sin and your need for a Savior, trusting that He alone has finished the work the Father requires of us. As believers, we never outgrow our need for the gospel message that the life, death, and resurrection of Jesus is our only key to the kingdom.

Do you depend solely on Jesus and His finished work for your salvation? Or do you feel like your salvation depends on your actions, motives, family, or culture? Or even some combination of those options?

As JTB continued baptizing, a man of relative obscurity showed up on the scene and asked to be baptized. JTB had been telling anyone who would listen that the King was coming, and He had finally shown up! JTB recognized Him as the King and also recognized the irony of a sinless Man asking to be baptized.

What did Jesus mean when He told JTB that His baptism was "fitting for us to fulfill all righteousness" (Matthew 3:15)? Use a Bible commentary if it's helpful.

Jesus didn't need to be baptized as a confession of sin, but to identify with the broken and fallen people He came to save. According to some faith traditions, He was also purifying the water for all those who would be baptized into the kingdom. And the entire Trinity was on hand to set His baptism apart from the rest!

Review 3:16–17. What distinct roles did the three persons of the Trinity (Father, Son, Spirit) play in Jesus's baptism?

Father _____

Son _____

Spirit _____

Why is it important that Jesus's mission wasn't a solo one?

As followers of Jesus, we recognize that we contribute nothing to our salvation except the sin that Jesus died for. It's in His death and resurrection that we're given the Holy Spirit to dwell within us, giving us direct access to the Father and all of His wisdom, strength, and love. The three work together in unison to help us live for the glory of the King!

Matthew 4:1–11

 READ MATTHEW 4:1–11

Just as Jesus identified with those He came to save by stepping into the waters of baptism, He also experienced the types of temptation that are common to humanity, but in the most extreme forms. You'd think that after such a celebratory commissioning with the entire Trinity, Jesus would have momentum to dive into active ministry. But instead of launching into the spotlight, He was led by the Spirit into a more private experience—a forty-day wilderness fast that ended with a series of temptations.

Read James 1:13. What is the difference between being led to a place where temptation will happen and being the source of temptation?

Why would the Holy Spirit lead Jesus to a place of temptation?

Using a dictionary, look up the definition of *temptation*. **How is it different from sin?**

Read 1 Corinthians 10:13. What does it say about temptation?

This passage (1 Corinthians 10:13) is often misquoted, suggesting God won't give us more than we can handle—which isn't true. In fact, Scripture regularly tells us that we'll most certainly face situations that are well beyond our strength and that we'll need to depend on the King in radical ways. Instead, what this passage reveals is that Jesus personally knows what temptation is like, and He can always equip you to choose not to sin if you'll rely on His strength.

Before Christ's temptation by the devil, He spent forty days fasting in a desert wilderness. Even with the Holy Spirit sustaining Him through the fast, Jesus was hungry at the end. Biologically, the return of hunger pangs after a long fast indicates that death isn't far off. This is the setting where we find Jesus when the tempter arrives on the scene with three temptations.

Read 1 John 2:16. What three categories of temptation does the world provide?

- _____
- _____
- _____

Each of the three temptations Jesus faced falls within a different one of those categories. Hebrews 2:18 and 4:15 tell us that Jesus was tempted in every way, yet He never sinned. But Jesus is more than just an example for us to follow—He's the one who fulfilled all righteousness because He knows we never could (Matthew 3:15)!

Which of the three temptation categories does temptation number one (Matthew 4:3) fit into?

In temptation number one, how does Jesus's response (quoting Deuteronomy 8:3) address "desires of the flesh" for both His situation and our own moments of temptation?

Which of the three categories does temptation number two (Matthew 4:5–6) fit into?

What was the devil trying to get Jesus to do in temptation number two? Use a Bible commentary if it's helpful.

Interestingly, the devil quoted Psalm 91:11–12 in his temptation of Jesus. The enemy knows God's Word inside and out, but he didn't quote it with reverence. Instead, he pulled two verses out of context as a means of manipulation and personal gain. Unfortunately, Scripture is often used in this way, even within Christendom. That's why resources like this book, *The Bible Recap*, Bible study and discipleship groups, and others are so important. When we don't know what the Bible actually says, we're not armed to fight lies and temptations with the truth.

In temptation number two, how does Jesus's response (quoting Deuteronomy 6:16) address the appeal to the pride of life?

Which of the three categories does temptation number three (Matthew 4:8–9) fit into?

In His last reply, Jesus told Satan, "Be gone!", then used a phrase from the Old Testament that shows up in four different places (Deuteronomy 6:13–14 and 10:20; Joshua 24:14; 1 Samuel 7:3). Jesus wasn't messing around—He was using repeated truth because it bears repeating. "'You shall worship the Lord your God and him only shall you serve.'" Israel needed to hear it repeated and we need to hear it repeated. It's a powerful reminder to the enemy that we have one God, and it's not him!

Why do you think Jesus used Scripture to battle temptation? How is this an example for us?

Of the three categories of temptations that 1 John 2:16 outlines, which do you find most difficult to battle?

Find and write out three verses that relate to your specific temptation. (OpenBible.Info/Topics is a great place to look if you need help.)

When Tempted

Verse	
Verse	
Verse	

Verse 11 tells us the devil left and the angels came and took care of Jesus. We see not only Jesus's victory, but God's provision. It's a great reminder that He won't leave us to fend for ourselves in the midst of our temptation. The next time you find yourself struggling with your primary temptation, remember the verses you wrote above and speak the truth of God's Word to the enemy and to yourself!

Matthew 4:12–25

READ MATTHEW 4:12-25

After hearing about the imprisonment of his friend and cousin JTB, Jesus moved from His hometown of Nazareth to a town near the Sea of Galilee. And—you guessed it—yet another prophecy from Isaiah was fulfilled! Isaiah 9:1–2 suggests that the people in Galilee, including Gentiles, would see the light dawning—and the Light Himself dawned on them indeed!

Look at verse 17. Write out Jesus's first words of preaching below. Underline the word of action Jesus emphasized to His hearers.

Look up the verses listed in the table below. Write the name of the person speaking. Then write the name of the person or people they were calling to repentance.

Passage	Speaker	Called to Repentance
Matthew 3:2		
Mark 6:12		
Acts 2:38		
Acts 26:19–20		
Revelation 2:5		

What does the repetition of this message throughout Scripture tell you about the heart of God?

While in the Galilee region, Jesus called His first followers—a handful of young men who were fishing along the shoreline outside Capernaum. Imagine being hard at work in the family business, thinking it's probably all you'll ever know, when a rabbi (teacher) named Jesus shows up and invites you to follow Him. Jewish boys often began following a rabbi around age twelve, but it's possible these followers were a few years older—likely between the ages of thirteen to fifteen—since they were already working but still young enough to take up the opportunity of rabbi-following.

Review 4:18–22 and answer the following questions:

Name the two pairs of brothers and their occupation.

What was each pair doing when they were called?

What did Jesus call them to? Why do you think He used a fishing analogy?

What was their response to the call and vision Jesus set before them?

What did they leave behind to follow Jesus? What is the significance of each?

It's interesting to note that they weren't perpetually sitting at home, hours deep into their favorite streaming service (or the first-century equivalent). They were hard at work, faithful to hone their craft so they could contribute to their families. These were not idle men. And their call from Jesus wasn't to "check something out" to see if it fit their schedule or personality. It was a full-time call to a life-on-life education from Rabbi Jesus. Leaving their profession and family wasn't just an opportunity to try something new, it was a deep commitment to a completely new identity. They'd no longer be defined as fishermen, but as disciples of the King.

Though not all believers are called to leave our occupations and move away from our families for vocational ministry, we *are* called to identify first and foremost as followers of Jesus in the places God has put us. We can find identities in a lot of incredible things—we just need to be mindful that our first identity impacts the way we function in our other identities (parent, sibling, employee, athlete, etc.).

What aspects of your identity have the potential to displace your primary identity as a disciple of the King?

Describe someone in your vocational field who authentically represents their identity as a Christ-follower first.

What adjustments do you want to make so that your primary identity is found in your position as a disciple of the King?

Jesus and His followers went throughout the region of Galilee, teaching and proclaiming the gospel of the kingdom and healing diseases and afflictions of all kinds—including demonic oppression!

Why do you think "proclaiming the gospel of the kingdom" is listed before His healings and miraculous works?

What do you think caused His fame to spread and prompt great crowds to follow Him?

As Jesus's ministry is officially inaugurated, two groups of people form. The first are those willing to leave behind all that identifies them in order to follow and be formed by Jesus and His words. The second are those who are tracking His movements, looking for what Jesus can give them or do for them.

Jesus was and is looking for people who are eager to walk in a completely new identity as His followers. While other identities may bring temporary happiness, life in the eternal kingdom of Jesus will be abundantly more fulfilling now and for eternity, because He's where the joy is!

What stood out to you most in this week's study? Why?

What did you learn or relearn about God and His character this week?

Corresponding Psalm & Prayer

 READ PSALM 2

What correlation do you see between Psalm 2 and this week's study of Jesus and His kingdom?

What portions of this psalm stand out to you most?

Close by praying this prayer aloud:

Father,

I praise You for being God over all the nations. Jesus, You are the King over all kings! Thank You for the blessing of taking refuge in You.

Father, I have sinned. Both John the Baptist and Jesus preached the message of repentance, so I know there is hope for me to turn from my sins. I repent of my sins and turn to You and ask You to make my heart clean. I confess that I have raged and plotted in vain. Like the wicked kings in Scripture, I've tried to forge my own paths instead of submitting to Your kingship and Your kingdom. Like King Herod, I've wanted to maintain my power instead of worshiping You.

You have shown me great mercy. Help me to extend Your mercy to others. As I face temptation, empower me to preach the truth to myself and to the enemy of my soul. Equip me with the truths from Your Word so that I can either stand strong or flee—and give me wisdom to know which is needed at the time. Help me walk in humility with my eyes fixed on Your Son Jesus and His kingdom.

I surrender my life to You, Lord—every moment of my day, each decision I make, I yield my will and way to Your perfect will and way.

I love You too. Amen.

Rest, Catch Up, or Dig Deeper

 WEEKLY CHALLENGE

You may have a lineage marked by dysfunction and pain, or perhaps you have a legacy of faith and devotion. Regardless of where your family lies on the spectrum, it's helpful to look back on your life and your story as you think about the future. God has been and is at work in your story—or you wouldn't be sitting here studying His Word today!

Make a family tree of your family as far back as you'd like (even if all you have access to is your current generation) and make a list of areas where you see God's redemption at play.

How does looking back help inform what you'd like to see in future generations?

Matthew 5–7:
Message of the King

DAILY BIBLE READING

Day 1: Matthew 5:1–16

Day 2: Matthew 5:17–48

Day 3: Matthew 6:1–18

Day 4: Matthew 6:19–34

Day 5: Matthew 7

Day 6: Psalm 112

Day 7: Catch-Up Day

Corresponds to Day 283 of *The Bible Recap*.

WEEKLY CHALLENGE

See page 62 for more information.

Matthew 5:1–16

READ MATTHEW 5:1–16

Early in His ministry, Jesus, surrounded by His disciples, sat on a hillside near the Sea of Galilee to deliver His most famous sermon, the Sermon on the Mount. He began by listing eight blessings.

Look up the word *blessed* (5:3) in a Greek lexicon and write down what you find. What other meaning(s) does this word have?

Most often, the word means something close to "happy," but the irony is that the things Jesus offered as the means to this happiness don't feel very happy to us—things like mourning, hunger, persecution. Yet His words surely would've been a balm to His audience. They were primarily Jewish people in a rural, agrarian society, living under the oppression of the Roman army, who had seized control of their nation. He was offering them a better hope beyond this life. He was offering them something that felt somewhat backward. The path to inheriting the earth is to be *meek*? That feels at odds with human nature, doesn't it?

And that's exactly what Jesus was establishing. As King of the kingdom of heaven, Jesus was helping them understand that things in His kingdom are upside-down. We see it in 5:3 and 5:10—spiritual poverty and persecution are the path to inheriting the kingdom. You must be poor to be rich. Everything about the kingdom of God feels like a threat to our sensibilities.

Review Matthew 5:3. Who will be blessed? In your own words, describe what it means to be "poor in spirit," or spiritually poor.

Spiritual poverty is recognizing that we have nothing to offer God, no reason for Him to choose us or love us. And if we get really honest about it, we aren't just empty-handed—we don't show up with zero dollars in our account—we're in debt. Despite how backward that sounds or how much that offends our pride and sense of self-worth, God says *that* is the starting point. Spiritual poverty is square one. We cannot participate in the kingdom of heaven without recognizing our desperate need for God.

As we look at these blessings, it's interesting to consider that they might not be *only* a list—they might be a *cumulative* list. If that's true, then this first blessing is the foundation of the entire sermon.

As you read through the types of people who receive the blessings Jesus listed (e.g., the poor in spirit, those who mourn, the meek, etc.), which descriptions seem to apply most to you? Which might not apply to you right now?

For those of us in the kingdom, the King's impact on our lives should bless others—even those who aren't in the kingdom. Verses 13–14 say the "earth" and the "world" will benefit from us knowing God.

Is there someone in your life who doesn't know Jesus as King who benefits from your relationship with Him?

Review Matthew 5:16. Jesus said He wants others to see our light shining. Who did He say should receive the glory when others see our good works?

Matthew 5:17–48

 **READ MATTHEW 5:17-48**

It's easy for us to turn the Sermon on the Mount into a checklist. Whether we feel like we're nailing it or blowing it, both of those vantage points are still focusing on *us* being the ones to get it right. Then, without even realizing it, we're back at the start again, needing to be reminded of our spiritual poverty. Neither of those places represents spiritual poverty. It's vital to remember that on our best days and on our worst days, our only hope is the cross of Christ.

When it comes to your relationship with God and the world around you, are you more tempted to focus on your wins (what you're doing well) or your losses (what you're doing poorly)?

Review Matthew 5:20. What is required for entering the kingdom of heaven? **Compare this to Jesus's words in 5:3.** How can both of these things be true?

Reflect on the Ten Commandments and the other Old Testament laws Jesus referenced in 5:17–48. What did Jesus repeatedly reveal about God's standards for holiness?

Jesus didn't say, "You'll never be able to keep God's law, so God's going to lower the bar. Just do whatever you want and God will be okay with it, because He's a God of love." Instead, He pointed out that God isn't just after right actions—He's after a right heart. If you don't murder anyone but you hate everyone around you, that doesn't echo God and His love to a fallen world, and it doesn't feel like freedom. The King, on the other hand, values reconciliation and peace, and He encourages humility in pursuing those things.

When Jesus talked about lust, He touched on ideas that show up in the Old Testament as well, revealing that God has always cared about not only our actions but our hearts too.

Read Exodus 20:17. How does this commandment reveal that God has always cared about what's happening in our hearts?

God's standard has not changed. It's possible to do a good deed out of a wicked motive, but God requires that both heart and action be pure. In Amos 5:21–24, God told His people that He hated their good deeds because they were done out of an impure heart that denied justice and ignored righteousness.

While we will all sin in many ways, a pure heart will prompt us to take action against falling into future sin. Jesus used strong hyperbolic language (cut off your hand, pluck out your eye) to illustrate this. He spoke of standards that seemed too high for most people: esteeming marriage, doing what you say you will, and having honor that is higher than an oath. He called His people to love their enemies and forgo retaliation. Again, He revealed that His kingdom is an upside-down kingdom—one of humility, generosity, and kindness.

Ask God to bring to mind anyone who could be considered your enemy or persecutor. In keeping with 5:44, pray a blessing over them. Ask God to help you *mean it* so that you're not just doing the right action, but setting your heart right as well.

Today's reading closes with these shocking words of Jesus: "You therefore must be perfect, as your heavenly Father is perfect" (5:48). Perfection is what God requires. That feels exhausting at best, impossible at worst.

Look up the word *perfect* (5:48) in a Greek lexicon and write down what you find. What other meaning(s) does this word have?

It's helpful to know that the word *perfect* here carries the idea of being "complete." Our only hope of being perfected or completed is by receiving the righteousness Christ grants us. That's why it's such great news that Jesus hasn't come to abolish the law but to fulfill it (see 5:17). He has completed the requirements of the law through His perfect life and perfect death.

Second Corinthians 5:21 says, "For our sake he made him to be sin who knew no sin, so that in him we might become the righteousness of God." This is how it can be true that we are spiritually bankrupt (Matthew 5:3), yet our righteousness meets His standards (5:20, 5:48). It's only because Christ has fully paid our debt through His death on the cross *and* the righteousness He attained has been assigned to us!

Matthew 6:1–18

READ MATTHEW 6:1-18

Jesus continued casting vision for what kingdom life looks like: Our actions should be motivated by a desire to please God, not others. He challenged our natural desire to earn respect or establish a reputation through good deeds.

The Pharisees were a group of strict religious leaders in Jesus's day, and they often acted in ways that put the focus on themselves. Jesus used an interesting word to describe them; He called them *hypocrites*—this was the word for Greek actors in Jesus's day. These actors held up different masks over their faces depending on which role they were playing. This was a fitting word choice for the Pharisees since they were putting on a performance, doing showy acts in front of others.

Instead of condemning the action altogether, Jesus gave a series of clear directives, saying, "Do the thing they're doing, but don't do it *that* way" followed by "Do it *this* way instead." He pointed to a more discreet method, and while it may not eradicate the selfish motive entirely, it can deal a healthy blow to the ego. Be generous to the needy, He said, but without fanfare. Pray, but not to gain attention. Fast, but without making a public show of it. In all these actions, it's important to remember "square one"—our spiritual poverty. We don't bring anything to the table except our sin and our great need for Him.

Write Ephesians 2:10 below. Find who this verse credits with preparing our good works, then circle that name.

Read Philippians 2:12–13, then write verse 13 below. Find who this verse credits with giving us the desire to do good works and accomplishing them through us, then circle that name.

How do you feel as you read these verses? How does this truth impact your thoughts about God? How does it impact your thoughts about your actions?

Our good deeds—giving, praying, fasting—are beautiful things that glorify God and bring us joy as we participate in them. He delights in you as you give, pray, and fast! And it's important to remember that it's not bad to *be seen* doing these things; it's just bad to do these things *to be seen*. For instance, maybe your community serves the poor together, or perhaps someone asks you to lead a group in prayer, or maybe you're enduring a lengthy fast and you want to ask your community to pray for you. God is honored in those things!

Review Matthew 6:6 and 6:9. Who did Jesus instruct His followers to pray to? Is this who you normally address your prayers to? Why or why not?

Jesus drilled down on prayer when He taught His disciples how to pray. He gave them a template that is both theologically dense and simple enough to stand on its own. He instructed His followers to talk to the Father and to have a real, humble, relational conversation. Praying to Jesus or the Spirit isn't wrong, but it isn't what we typically see happening in God's Word. The typical way we see prayer modeled in Scripture is to pray to the Father, through the Son, by the Spirit. That can be challenging for those of us with terrible (or absent) earthly fathers or with misguided views of our heavenly Father. We may prefer to talk to Jesus because He seems more relatable. But Jesus reminded His followers that the Father hears them and will generously respond to their prayers.

As for fasting, Jesus spoke of it as an assumed part of their lives—saying *when* you fast, not *if* you fast. In biblical terms, fasting always pertained to abstaining from food and was always tied to prayer. Secular scientists commend the physical benefits of fasting, but Scripture's approach to fasting brings the Christian a full realm of benefits—physical, mental, emotional, and spiritual.

In all of today's discussion of spiritual disciplines, Jesus emphasized two connected themes about God. The phrase *in secret* shows up six times, reiterating that God is engaged with the things of the heart—He's there, He knows what's happening, He sees it all. And the word *reward* shows up seven times, the text always listing God as the giver of the reward.

Read Hebrews 11:6. Who is rewarded? Why?

Who gives the reward?

How does this inform your view of the Father?

How does this shape your view of the importance of prayer?

Tomorrow we'll look into how believing these truths about God will help us lean into love and put fear to death.

Matthew 6:19–34

 **READ MATTHEW 6:19-34**

In today's section of the Sermon on the Mount, Jesus repeatedly connected our values to our worries.

Write out the four verses where Jesus instructed His followers about something He didn't want them to do.

6:19—Do not _____

6:25—Do not _____

6:31—Do not _____

6:34—Do not _____

If we obey the "do not store up" of verse 19 (NIV), then the "do not be anxious" of verses 25, 31, and 34 will naturally follow, because our hearts will be anchored in things that are eternal, not things that are fleeting.

Fear is connected to our values and our identity. Where you find your identity determines what you value. What you value determines what you fear losing or never having. What you fear losing or never having will almost certainly prompt fear and striving if it takes up too much space in your heart.

If you find your identity in the fleeting things, fear is very natural. But if you find your identity in the eternal things—in His kingdom—fear itself becomes the fleeting thing.

We can learn to grow in faith. We can learn to push back against our fears. We can learn to adjust what we value. The way we do that is by getting to know God more, reading His Word, seeing His character, and learning to trust Him. As we do that, we'll learn more about what He values and we can ask Him to help us value those things too.

The problem with trying to be rich in what the world values is that it's all Monopoly money anyway. It can't earn you anything except tiny plastic hotels on a piece of cardboard that will end up at a thrift store someday. Jesus effectively told His disciples, *Stop trying to get more plastic hotels. Enough with the Monopoly money! Fix your time, emotion, and effort on something that will last.* In 6:21, He said it this way: "Where your treasure is, there your heart will be also." Heart follows treasure. What you invest your time, money, and emotion into is what you'll really value.

Take a minute to pause and get honest with yourself: What percentage of your time and emotion is spent on things of eternal value? In a very practical sense, how might you spend more of your time on things that have eternal value?

If the percentage (in your answer to the question above) is low, this is not an opportunity to shame yourself for it—it's an invitation into a life of greater freedom and joy. If we begin to value the eternal things above all else, then our concerns about the temporary things will take their rightful place. Of course we will always have earthly concerns, but it can be helpful to view those in light of eternity.

As Jesus taught these principles, He was likely talking to a group of people who were legitimately poor. He addressed their very real concerns about provision with reminders of who the Father is. He said it's normal for people who don't know God as their Father to be concerned about things like food and clothes; but for God's kids, Jesus said, "Remember how much the Father loves you! Remember how He values you above everything else He's created. That should free your heart up to focus on the things that truly matter, instead of things that are temporary. As long as you're focused on those fleeting things, you'll be filled with fear."

Jesus was serious about teaching His people not to fear. Fear usurps our allegiance to His kingdom. It fixes our eyes on the wrong things. It never stops demanding our attention. Instead, Jesus called us to remember who our Father is! He is providing for us!

In what areas of your life do you regularly encounter fear? Where do you find yourself striving? Read through today's passage again and write down the quotes from Jesus that speak to you the most.

Matthew 7

 READ MATTHEW 7

Look up the word *judge* **(7:1) in a Greek lexicon** and write down what you find. What other meaning(s) does this word have?

Review 7:1–5, which warns of judging. **Then review 7:15–20,** which seems to encourage it. On the surface, these two ideas seem to contradict each other, but how might they work together?

In verses 1–5, Jesus tells us not to judge others, but in verses 15–20, He seems to be telling us *to* judge others—to discern whether someone is bearing healthy or diseased fruit. Here are three bits of information that are helpful in understanding how these two ideas work together.

First, God is the judge of all mankind (Genesis 18:25). He hands down the verdict and its very real consequences. Humans don't have that power, nor should we, because we don't know people's hearts like God does (Psalm 139:1–4, Jeremiah 11:20). If this were a courtroom setting, we'd be in the audience, not holding the gavel. It's technically impossible for us to be the ones to pronounce eternal judgment.

Second, what we often refer to as "judging"—the kind humans *can* do—is better defined as "approving or disapproving." We don't have the power to condemn someone to hell. Jesus was saying, "Don't try to weigh someone's heart, because you don't actually know it. By presuming you can, you're presuming to be God, which is in itself worthy of condemnation." Jesus also reminded us that our own sin gets in the way of viewing others clearly (7:4–5).

Third, Jesus calls us to be fruit inspectors (verses 15–20), which is altogether different from the types of judging we just described. We can inspect the fruit, but we can't see its roots, and we aren't the ones who chop the tree down. We need to be discerning because we don't want to eat bad fruit. In the big farmers' market of religious teachers and spiritual gurus, there's a lot of rotten fruit. It may look glossy on the outside, but if it doesn't measure up to Scripture, we shouldn't seek it for nutrition. It's also worth noting that there's a difference between a *bruised* apple and an apple that's full of *worms or disease*. While some fruit is diseased or deadly, other fruit may only have minor flaws.

Jesus calls for humility and wisdom. He wasn't saying judgment won't happen—it's coming for all of us—and He wasn't saying, "To each their own!" But God's judgment happens at a heart level, and we don't have eyes to see that, so it's best to direct our discernment toward an action being right or wrong instead of a person being good or bad. When we venture into that territory, we lose sight of square one: our own spiritual poverty. Square one isn't a spot we move on from, leave behind, or outgrow—it's the foundation everything else is built on.

Which is harder for you—not judging others or being a discerning fruit inspector? Why? Ask God to help you grow in wisdom and humility so you can rightly hold the tension of both directives.

In 7:7–11, we see how the Father has a heart of generosity toward His kids. He listens. He cares. He gives good gifts. And He invites us to ask for what we want!

Using the ESV, KJV, NIV, CSB, or AMP translation of the Bible, reread 7:12. Write the first word of the verse here:

By opening this verse with this word, Jesus connected it to the previous verses, showing cause and effect. *Because* we have a generous Father who hears us, cares, and is generous toward us, we can extend that same kindness to others. We can give what we have received from Him.

Which is harder for you—asking God for things for yourself or being generous toward others? Why? How might this connection between the two help you grow in the area where you're weaker?

After Jesus talked about being a fruit inspector, He said many people have what appears to be good fruit but still don't know Him as their King and Savior. Calling Him "Lord" and doing miracles isn't the way into the kingdom. As always, God is after more than just good words and deeds—He's after our hearts! The kingdom is for people with *new hearts*.

A morally upright person who identifies as a Christian may seem to be in the kingdom, but through time and life's storms, their foundation will be revealed. Have they built their house on the rock that is King Jesus? Or on the sand? As beneficial as it may be, living a good, moral life can't save you. Both hedonism and morality are sand. Rock is *relationship*. Rock is *heart change.* If your life isn't built on knowing God, all your kingdoms are sandcastles.

As Jesus taught these words, people recognized that He had a unique authority. The scribes they were used to hearing primarily quoted others or posed questions without answers. Jesus, on the other hand, spoke like He had authority over the text. And He does, because He *is* the Word (John 1:1, 14). He's where the truth is, and He's where the joy is!

What stood out to you most in this week's study? Why?

What did you learn or relearn about God and His character this week?

Corresponding
Psalm & Prayer

 READ PSALM 112

What correlation do you see between Psalm 112 and this week's study of Jesus and His kingdom?

What portions of this psalm stand out to you most?

Close by praying this prayer aloud:

Father,
*   I praise You for the way You've provided for me and protected me. Thank You for Your Word and Your commands—it's a blessing to get to know You better through reading Your Word. Thank You*

for knowing all my needs and yet still inviting me to ask You for my desires.

Father, I have sinned, and I appeal to Your mercy. I repent of my sins and turn to You and ask You to make my heart clean. I confess that I'm given to striving and fearing. I confess that I want to build my own kingdom sometimes instead of submitting to Your kingship and Your kingdom. But because of Your Spirit at work in me, I have new eyes to see, new ears to hear, and a new heart to love You!

You have been generous to me. Help me to extend Your generosity to others, to bless the poor in the ways You have blessed me. Grant me a heart that is firm and steady, that I might not be fearful of bad news. Fix my eyes on You and Your eternal kingdom, not the fleeting things.

I surrender my life to You, Lord—every moment of my day, each decision I make, I yield my will and way to Your perfect will and way.

I love You too. Amen.

Rest, Catch Up, or Dig Deeper

 WEEKLY CHALLENGE

Our weekly challenge comes from our reading on Day 2. In 5:29–30, Jesus said, "If your right eye causes you to sin, tear it out and throw it away. For it is better that you lose one of your members than that your whole body be thrown into hell. And if your right hand causes you to sin, cut it off and throw it away. For it is better that you lose one of your members than that your whole body go into hell."

As mentioned previously, Jesus used hyperbolic language—cut off your hand, pluck out your eye—to demonstrate how the pure in heart will take action against falling into future sin.

Journal through these questions: What are your weak spots? What sin traps do you repeatedly fall into? What practical steps can you take to avoid falling into those traps? Be specific. Who can you confess this struggle to and ask for prayer or accountability?

As you seek to address these areas in your life, resist despair! Even if you've failed ten thousand times, and even if you fail again this week, remember what we learned on Day 2 about our perfection—it comes from Jesus and His righteous acts, not our own. He has already accomplished all that the Father requires of us!

Matthew 8–10:
Authority of the King

DAILY BIBLE READING

Day 1: Matthew 8:1–17
Day 2: Matthew 8:18–34
Day 3: Matthew 9
Day 4: Matthew 10:1–25
Day 5: Matthew 10:26–42
Day 6: Psalm 8
Day 7: Catch-Up Day

Corresponds to Days 280, 284, and 289 of *The Bible Recap*.

WEEKLY CHALLENGE

See page 86 for more information.

DAY 1

Matthew 8:1–17

◣ **READ MATTHEW 8:1–17**

After Jesus finished delivering His sermon outlining life in the kingdom, many of the people in the crowd decided to follow Him. Some of them surely thought He was crazy, some likely thought He was deceiving everyone, and others may have believed Him to be the promised Messiah.

As they came down the mountain, a leper approached Jesus, knelt in front of Him, and asked for healing. The leper's humility is evident. He didn't approach Jesus with entitlement or demands—he knelt and he asked. He demonstrated one of the very points Jesus made in the message He'd just finished teaching (7:7–11). It's possible the leper had been on the fringes of the crowd and heard Him deliver this message of God's great generosity. If so, this would've been not only an act of faith but an act of obedience!

When you're in desperate need for Jesus to work on your behalf, what is your heart posture toward Him?

What posture do you think the King of kings holds toward you in the midst of your needs?

Review 8:3. What do you notice about Jesus's response to the leper?

With compassion, Jesus stretched out His hand to the leper. As King of His creation, He knew He had authority over illness and that He wouldn't be made unclean because of this man's skin disease. He spoke to the outcast leper and granted his request, then He told him to keep quiet. This hush-hush behavior is often referred to as the "messianic secret," which simply refers to Jesus's desire to wait to reveal His identity as Messiah until the proper time. Even though great crowds were already gathering, Jesus had a specific purpose and timeline to walk out, and He didn't want to draw more attention to Himself. However, He did want the priest to be informed of the healing, in keeping with the law (Leviticus 13–14). Being healed from leprosy was a big deal. In the Old Testament, only two people were healed of leprosy—Miriam (Numbers 12:1–15) and the Gentile Naaman (2 Kings 5:14).

Read 2 Kings 5. Note the differences between how the king of Israel handled Naaman and how King Jesus handled the leper.

Next, Jesus entered Capernaum, a fishing village where both Jews and Gentiles lived. A Roman leader approached Him and explained that his servant was paralyzed and "suffering terribly" (v. 6). Despite the fact that this Roman centurion was both a Gentile and an enemy of Israel, Jesus offered to come and heal his servant.

What do the centurion's words in verses 8–9 reveal about his view of Jesus?

The centurion knew what Jesus was capable of. Jesus was amazed by his faith, and He used this moment not only to praise this Gentile's faith but to teach His followers that those without faith won't enter the kingdom of heaven—regardless of whether they are Jews or Gentiles. Jesus emphasized that even "the sons of the kingdom"—a term for the nation of Israel—will be cast into darkness if they don't believe in Him. After this teaching, Jesus performed His first long-distance healing. King Jesus has the authority to command sickness to flee, even from far away.

From there, Jesus went to Peter's house, where his sick mother-in-law was lying in bed. When Jesus touched her, the fever left her, and she got up immediately. She didn't need time to recover from her sickness after being weak in bed. She was fully restored right away. And when she got up, she didn't just resume her daily tasks. Instead, she took time to serve the One who made her well.

Take time to list moments in your life when God's action was vital. Write a simple prayer thanking Him for all He has done.

Matthew 8:18–34

◥ READ MATTHEW 8:18–34

Jesus didn't send out His disciples to gather large crowds. He didn't need a hype man or a marketing team. The crowds often found Him, but in this instance, Jesus didn't stay with the crowd. Instead, He announced that He and His disciples would be going to the other side of the lake. This "other side" was the Gentile side, where the non-Jews lived—an unclean place that followers of God intentionally avoided. True to form, Jesus stepped outside of another cultural comfort zone and called His disciples to follow Him there. When He gave these bold orders, two men approached Him with questions about following Him.

Compare and contrast the scribe (8:19) and the disciple (8:21). What did Jesus's responses indicate about what it means to follow Him?

Both men desired to follow Jesus. One was eager without fully counting the cost; the other was willing, but only after his affairs were in order. Following King Jesus means giving Him full allegiance. No other kings reign in our life—not comfort, money, or relationships.

Jesus and His committed disciples climbed into the boat to begin their trip. This fishing boat was nothing like a luxury yacht or your uncle's pontoon boat. The typical first-century Galilean fishing boat was roughly twenty-seven feet long, seven feet wide, and four feet tall. When a fragile boat like that encountered the spontaneous storms that often occurred on the Galilee, it was enough to make the most experienced fishermen shake in their sandals. Yet in the midst of this chaos, the King of creation was asleep.

Read the following passages: Colossians 1:15–18, Hebrews 1:3, Psalm 65, and Psalm 89:9. Write down the phrases that highlight Jesus's authority over creation.

Colossians 1:15–18	
Hebrews 1:3	
Psalm 65	
Psalm 89:9	

In the span of a few moments, Jesus's disciples witnessed both His humanity as He slept and His deity as He commanded creation to obey Him. Jesus is the image of the invisible God, eternally begotten, ruling and reigning over all creation—which He created. When He spoke, the waves didn't just diminish, they disappeared. The disciples were amazed at the great calm.

Review 8:26. Where did Jesus direct His rebuke? What does this reveal about Jesus?

Matthew 8:18-34 | 69

The phrase *little faith* in this verse appears to be a word Jesus invented. Every time it shows up in Scripture, Jesus was the one saying it, and it isn't found in any secular writing from that time. He used this phrase exclusively with His followers (those of *little* faith, as opposed to those of *no* faith) and most often with the disciples specifically. The context makes it appear as though it's a gentle nickname meant to encourage them to have more faith in Him. He does not appear to be rebuking them in this passage, but encouraging them. This story seems to show that Jesus didn't rebuke His disciples for their fear. Instead, He rebuked the *source* of their fear.

What fears are you currently facing? How would Jesus rebuke those fears and comfort you in the midst of them?

The disciples were amazed and relieved that the storm ceased, but little did they know, they were about to encounter a different type of threat—the spiritual forces of darkness!

Review 8:29–31. **How did the demons react when Jesus arrived at the tombs?**

The demons recognized Jesus immediately and knew He had authority to destroy them. They knew their final fate would be eternal torment. They asked, "Have you come to torment us *before the time*?" With one word, Jesus cast them into a herd of pigs and the pigs ran into the sea. Surprisingly, the crowd didn't celebrate the demons being gone and the men being set free. Instead, they were livid about the death of thousands of pigs, which were a major source of income in their agrarian society.

As news spread about what happened, the locals begged Jesus to leave. Two men were finally free, but the people were focused on what was lost. Their value system was revealed and it stood in stark contrast to God's. The people in the land of the Gadarenes wanted nothing to do with Jesus or His upside-down kingdom.

Which of your values are in contrast with God's value system? Where does this create tension in your life?

What I Value	What God Values	Tension

Matthew 9

◣ READ MATTHEW 9

After the crowds in the Gaderenes drove Jesus out, He and His disciples returned home to Capernaum. Everywhere He went, people needed His healing, and home was no exception. The next person He healed was a man who couldn't even come to Jesus on his own—his friends carried him there because he was paralyzed.

One of the things Jesus said to the man gives us a glimpse into his emotional state—Jesus told him, "Take heart." This phrase is used most often when someone has lost hope. While Jesus praised the friends for their faith, He didn't condemn the paralytic for lacking it. Instead, He spoke compassionately to him and forgave his sin. Jesus is a safe space for your hopelessness.

Why would Jesus declare the man's sins forgiven before addressing his physical need?

Jesus came to heal the broken, but even more, He came to fully redeem and restore *all* that is broken. This man wasn't paralyzed because he was a sinner, but his paralysis was a direct result of living in a sinful, broken world. With the scribes nearby, Jesus chose to demonstrate His power not only to heal the body but to forgive sins. In doing this, He gave His followers a preview of what He came to do for all of humanity: rescue us from our physical and spiritual brokenness. The Pharisees were aghast at Jesus's words and accused Him of blasphemy, but He knew their thoughts and addressed them.

Read Hebrews 4:12–13 and Psalm 139:1–2. How does Jesus's ability to know the scribes' thoughts prove He is God?

Only God can know the secret thoughts of men. Jesus, being fully God, knew. After He addressed the evil hearts of the Pharisees, He showed His authority over disability. The lame man walked! While the crowd rightfully acknowledged God's authority, they remained unable to acknowledge that Jesus was God.

What problem did the Pharisees have with Jesus's actions in 9:9–13? Summarize His response.

We've seen Jesus be drawn to those who are sick and destitute, but Matthew wasn't sick or destitute—in fact, he was healthy and wealthy enough to throw a dinner party. Matthew was definitely a sinner, and apparently that's what drew Jesus to him. Jesus referenced Hosea 6:6 and basically said, "Sinners are the whole reason I'm here."

How would you describe Jesus's interaction with the woman in 9:18–22?

King Jesus isn't distant. He doesn't rule and reign from afar. He isn't concerned only with the matters of important people like the ruler of the synagogue. He has always been willing to be interrupted by the least of these—including a woman whose issue of blood made her ceremonially unclean. An outcast for twelve years, she was destitute, desperate, and willing to risk everything to be healed.

Unlike some of the others we've read about, she didn't ask Jesus to heal her. She didn't cry out or draw attention to herself. Was she afraid of being a disruption or a bother? Fearful of being shamed, rejected, or silenced? Perhaps she held to only a thread of hope. She was accustomed to being overlooked, even by religious leaders, because she was unclean. But she carried a tenacious faith that prompted her to push past the social norms and *touch someone's clothes*. She didn't even try to touch Jesus Himself, which was forbidden because she could transmit her uncleanness. She could've been banished or stoned for such an audacious act. But Jesus turned to look at her, and when He spoke, she immediately knew He had healed her.

Are there any areas where you feel desperate or dismissed? List them below. Take time to pray through them, asking God for healing.

The King who came to save you and make you whole is the same King who sees you in all of your brokenness. He brings healing and shalom—wholeness. The greater your desperation for God, the greater your joy in being met by Him.

After healing the woman who had bled for twelve years, Jesus went to the ruler's house to heal his daughter. Although she was dead by the time He arrived, He took her hand and she stood. Just like with the bleeding woman, death had its own levels of uncleanness in Jewish law. But Jesus transformed the uncleanliness of death into purity—*new life*. For the first time in the book of Matthew, King Jesus displayed His authority over death. And that won't be the last time He demonstrates this reality of His kingship; in His kingdom, death doesn't win.

Describe the responses of the crowd and the Pharisees in 9:33–34.

After leaving the ruler's house, Jesus met two blind men, saw their faith, and healed them. Then, He and the disciples met a mute man affected by demons. Jesus cast the demons out, the man spoke, and the crowds marveled; but the Pharisees took the opportunity to plant rumors about Him. They essentially said, "Jesus can call the plays for the demons because He's the quarterback of their team." They saw Jesus's authority in His miracles and His teaching, but instead of praising Him as the long-awaited King, they accused Him of working for the Prince of Darkness.

As Jesus and His disciples traveled throughout the region and witnessed a wide variety of needs, He was "moved with compassion" (9:36 KJV). The word used for "moved with compassion" (*splagchnizomai*) is the strongest word for pity in the Greek language. But He didn't stop at merely feeling compassion—He leaned in with a call to action in response to the great need. King Jesus cares deeply for His people, and He knows the massive amount of work to be done for the kingdom. "The harvest is plentiful but the laborers are few" (9:37). The request for more workers is as urgent today as it was when Jesus first spoke these words.

In keeping with Jesus's orders to His followers in 9:38, "pray earnestly to the Lord of the harvest to send out laborers into his harvest." Write out your prayer below.

Matthew 10:1–25

◣◤ READ MATTHEW 10:1–25

In chapter 9, Jesus healed diseases, cast out a demon, and raised a dead person to life. At the end of that chapter, He urged His disciples to start *praying* for laborers; and this chapter opened with Jesus calling them to be the answer to their own prayer. Looking at Jesus's model, we see that He called a wide variety of people to be those laborers. In fact, the diversity of His closest followers was both mind-boggling and countercultural.

Grab a Bible dictionary, look up each of the twelve disciples, and fill in all the information you can find. (Note: You may not be able to fill in all the blanks.)

Disciple	Background (nationality/tribe)	Job
Simon (Peter)		
Andrew		
James		
John		
Philip		
Bartholomew		
Thomas		

Disciple	Background (nationality/tribe)	Job
Matthew		
James		
Thaddeus		
Simon (the Zealot)		
Judas Iscariot		

Within His small group of followers, Jesus enlisted people who would've been enemies, including a tax collector, who essentially betrayed his people to work for Rome, and a zealot, who wanted to overthrow Rome. These were staunch men who held opposite opinions about politics, national identity, and how those things applied to their lives. The disciples also ranged in education and financial status—not only did Jesus call a tax collector, but He also called blue-collar workers like fishermen. The upside-down kingdom is one where, despite their diversity, men and women are unified around the primary mission of the King.

Before Jesus sent them out on mission, He gave them authority to do the same things they'd watched Him do. But He didn't *only* give them authority—He also gave them specific instructions on how to wield that authority. They weren't empowered to do as they pleased; they were empowered to do the Father's will in accordance with His plan.

In 10:5–6, who does Jesus instruct the disciples to share the gospel with first? Why do you think He gave them this specific direction?

God's plan has always involved getting the message to the Jews first, then to the Gentiles, so Jesus's instruction was in keeping with this plan. In addition to giving them authority and instructions, Jesus also gave them limits. This would be their first mission, and it would require them to trust Him for every aspect of their provision and protection. When they first began following Jesus, they heard Him talk about God providing for even the birds and lilies (6:25–34); but as He sent them out, He charged them to demonstrate their belief that this was true for *them*. What was once a general concept had become a personal calling.

In 10:16–20, what kind of promise or warning did Jesus give them?

What animal did Jesus compare them to? Which two animals did He encourage them to imitate and in what ways?

Briefly describe how you might take on those traits in similar circumstances. What might that look like?

Jesus warned His followers that they would be mistreated, hated, and persecuted—much like He had been. He wanted to push the kingdom message out to places where it would be received and didn't want to waste time in areas where it would be rejected. He had practiced this kind of discernment in front of them—they'd seen Him navigate conversations differently based on whether He was talking with them, with Gentiles, or with the Pharisees. A serpent is wise enough to know when to assert itself and when to slip away. A dove can show up as a messenger of peace, or it can fly away and maintain its innocence. Together, wisdom and innocence help followers of Jesus know which battles to fight and which battles to forgo.

Who did Jesus say would go with the disciples to help them know how to respond to accusations?

Briefly describe a time when the Spirit helped or guided you. If you struggle to think of a time, recount His role in the story of your salvation (John 16:13).

Jesus reminded the disciples that God was not only the one calling them, but also the one equipping them. In fact, God the Spirit would be the one to speak *through* them! No matter what they faced, they wouldn't face it alone, so there was no need to be fearful.

He reminded them that the ones who endure to the end are the ones God has called and equipped—because what God initiates, He will sustain and He will fulfill. Being on mission with the King requires total dependence on Him to complete all He demands—we cannot do it in our own strength. And for every moment when we fail or fall short, we find rest in His finished work (John 19:30). It is the perfect, finished work of Jesus that saves us—not our own works—and it is the power of His Spirit that sustains our salvation (Titus 3:5–7).

Review 10:39. What has following Jesus cost you? Do you consider following Him worth the cost? Why or why not?

Matthew 10:26–42

READ MATTHEW 10:26–42

King Jesus continued His instructions to the disciples by telling them not to fear the challenges of the mission He was sending them on. In fact, He instructed them to climb up on a rooftop and boldly shout all the secrets of the kingdom that He'd been telling them behind closed doors. There was no place for fear in a mission like this—shouting from a rooftop takes guts!

Review 10:28. Use a Greek lexicon to look up the word *fear,* and write the three different definitions. How do these definitions shape this verse?

When it comes to the phrase *fear God*, a common misconception is that God's kids should be *afraid* of Him. But that's not at all what fearing God means. For those who know Him, the fear of the Lord looks a lot like reverence, delight, and awe. It draws us *to* God. For those who don't know Him, the other kind of fear is fitting, because His wrath remains on them (John 3:36). That kind of fear drives a person *away from* God.

As Jesus gave the assignment, He reminded His disciples that anything their enemies could do to them would be only temporary. He knew persecution would come, and He wanted them to be prepared, focused on the mission, and unwilling to yield to the threats and opinions of men.

Read Joshua 1:9, Deuteronomy 31:6, and Isaiah 41:10. What is the consistent command of God in each of these verses?

The enemy of your soul wants you to fear the mission *and* the One who sent you on the mission. Fear is crippling. It leaves us disempowered and hopeless. But King Jesus empowers us through His great love for us—eliminating fear of man and showing us how to rightly fear God.

What does rightly fearing God mean to you? When you approach God, which of the definitions of fear do you identify with most?

Jesus told His disciples that the only person they should fear was God, who *could* send them to hell, but who *wouldn't*, because they belonged to Him. In fact, Jesus said, God was attentive to their every move, keeping track of each hair on their head moment by moment. Jesus said He would talk to the Father about everyone who acknowledges Him as King (see also Hebrews 7:25). But for those who don't acknowledge Him as King, the thought of being outside of God's family *should* cause them to tremble.

Review 10:34–36, then go back and reread Matthew 5:9. How do you think both passages can be true?

The disciples may have been perplexed when their Teacher suddenly started saying He was bringing a sword. After all, in the Sermon on the Mount, He blessed the peacemakers, but here He was telling them He hadn't come to bring peace. Can you imagine the disciples scratching their heads, wondering, *Which one is it, Jesus—peacemaking or sword wielding? Make up Your mind!*

Read Ephesians 2:11–22. Summarize how King Jesus creates division while also bringing peace.

The message of Jesus is peace, but the radical mission of King Jesus has a way of creating division. Truly following the King means our devotion to Him must be over everything—family, occupation, political affiliation, denomination, nationality, *everything*. There is nothing higher than King Jesus. Jesus knew that His radical love for outsiders would offend many of those who were "insiders." Tearing down walls of hostility against the "others" in our world can create new walls and enemies even within our own households—people we love may take offense at our desire to love those who aren't like us. But for all those who rightly view King Jesus as supreme, unity follows—even across social divides. Division comes as a result of giving allegiance to anything other than the King.

Ask God to show you if there are things you've placed above Him in your life. What identities or opinions might cause unnecessary division between you and others in His kingdom? Write those things down. Repent.

For those who value Him above all else, Jesus promised rewards. He promised punishment for those who mistreat His kids and blessings for those who treat His kids well. King Jesus is a rewarder. Knowing Him is the greatest reward because He's where the joy is!

What stood out to you most in this week's study? Why?

What did you learn or relearn about God and His character this week?

Corresponding Psalm & Prayer

 READ PSALM 8

What correlation do you see between Psalm 8 and this week's study of Jesus and His kingdom?

What portions of this psalm stand out to you most?

Close by praying this prayer aloud:

Father,

Like the psalmist says, Your name is majestic indeed! I praise You for turning Your heart toward sinners like me. You are so loving and generous. You bring hope and healing to the leper, the demon possessed, the overlooked, the banished. And You have brought hope and healing to me! Thank You for being mindful of me and loving me so well.

Father, I have sinned, and I appeal to Your mercy. I confess that I've tried to establish my own strength and glory at times. I've tried to make a name for myself, to impress others, to win love—even Your love. I've valued my possessions and preferences over the things You value. I've forgotten that You have provided for me, protected me, and given me a place in Your kingdom through no effort or merit of my own. I repent of my sins and turn to You and ask You to make my heart clean.

Help me to walk in the glory and honor You've given me as Your child. May You be glorified. May You be honored.

I surrender my life to You, Lord—every moment of my day, each decision I make, I yield my will and way to Your perfect will and way.

I love You too. Amen.

Rest, Catch Up, or Dig Deeper

 WEEKLY CHALLENGE

In our reading this week, we saw Jesus's authority over nature, sickness, demons, and death. Jesus met people in their most desperate states and was moved with compassion. In order to love people compassionately like Jesus, we will need our eyes and hearts to look like His. His Spirit equips us for this good work!

This week, begin by writing out a short prayer in your journal, asking God to give you His heart and His eyes for those in need, to highlight specific people to you. It may be someone who is a social misfit or someone in obvious financial or physical need—or it may be someone who is a modern version of the rich young ruler.

As you begin to see people through the eyes of Jesus, write their names below your prayer in your journal, then set a prayer alarm on your phone as a reminder to pray for them at a specific time each day. As you pray, ask God how you should respond. It may be that God prompts you to take action in some way, but it may be that your prayers and your softened heart are the point (in other words, God may be changing *you* in this process because you will always be a person who needs the gospel too!). The primary goal in this challenge isn't to "fix" others, but to see our own hearts transformed so that we, too, will be moved with compassion like the King we follow.

┌ Scripture to Memorize ┐

And why are you anxious
about clothing? Consider
the lilies of the field,
how they grow: they
neither toil nor spin.

Matthew 6:28

Matthew 11–13:

Instructions of the King

DAILY BIBLE READING

Day 1: Matthew 11

Day 2: Matthew 12:1–32

Day 3: Matthew 12:33–50

Day 4: Matthew 13:1–33

Day 5: Matthew 13:34–58

Day 6: Psalm 84

Day 7: Catch-Up Day

Corresponds to Days 282, 285, and 287 of *The Bible Recap*.

WEEKLY CHALLENGE

See page 110 for more information.

Matthew 11

READ MATTHEW 11

Matthew 11 brings us back to John the Baptist (JTB), whom we haven't heard anything about since chapter four. All we know is he was put in prison just as Jesus was starting His ministry. JTB had been a faithful forerunner of Jesus, preaching repentance and pointing Israel to Him as their promised King. He prophetically rolled out the red carpet for Jesus and would've been eager to see Jesus's ministry take effect. But instead of getting to personally witness it, JTB had to patiently wait for updates from anyone who might've paid him a visit while he was in prison. These reports would've likely been the "highlight reel" of Jesus's activity in 4:12–11:1.

Skim 4:12–11:1 and summarize that portion of Jesus's ministry below.

If you were one of JTB's disciples, which event(s) would you have been sure to share with JTB?

While we don't know the specifics of what they told JTB, we do know that their reports left him with a pressing question for Jesus: "Are you the one who is to come, or shall we look for another?" JTB had been certain Jesus was "the coming One" and he wanted to confirm that he hadn't missed the mark.

Review 11:4–6. Then read Isaiah 35:5–6, 26:19, 29:18–19, and 61:1. Compare Jesus's response in Matthew to the prophecies from Isaiah. What do you notice? What is the significance of Jesus answering in this way?

Jesus's response may seem indirect, but JTB and other Jews who were well-versed in Scripture would've immediately recognized that Jesus was pointing to His ministry as the fulfillment of Old Testament prophecies about the Messiah. Jesus was undeniably declaring "The evidence speaks for itself. The search is over. I am the One."

There's a second, subtler message in His response that JTB wouldn't have missed either. When Jesus mentioned good news being preached to the poor, He was referencing Isaiah 61:1—but only the first part. Jesus left out the part about "the opening of the prison to those who are bound." JTB certainly would've noticed the missing portion and caught the heartbreaking message: "Yes, I'm the One, but you will die in prison."

How might the assurance that Jesus was the Messiah King have shaped JTB's perspective on his difficult circumstances?

Has the knowledge that Jesus is your King shaped your perspective on the challenging or heartbreaking circumstances in your life? If so, how?

After JTB's disciples left, Jesus turned His attention to the ever-present crowds. He held up JTB as an example of a prophet's job well done. JTB had been the reigning champ in human greatness up to that point, but from then on, even the last-place person in the kingdom could take that title. Jesus was revealing what an incredible honor it is to be included in the kingdom!

In the next bit of His message, Jesus spoke of dances and dirges, accusations of demon possession, and drunkards, and He denounced some significant cities. Jesus wasn't randomly ranting; He was making a cohesive point about Israel's lack of repentance and their rejection of Him. Even after witnessing His ministry and mighty works, they refused to acknowledge Him as King. Signs and miracles don't change hearts.

While Jesus had some sobering things to say, He didn't end the conversation with judgment and condemnation. In the final verses of the chapter, Jesus's tone took a turn toward gratitude. He thanked the Father for how He chooses to reveal things in His intentionally upside-down kingdom.

Review 11:25–30. What are some characteristics of a wise and understanding person? What are some characteristics of a person who is like a little child?

Next, Jesus did something we see in no other gospel account. He told us about His heart. Jesus wanted to leave no question as to who He is as a

King. He is compassionate and kind, gentle and lowly, and invites all who are longing for soul rest to come find it in His presence.

Review 11:25–30. Think about your testimony. How did God graciously reveal Himself to you? How has salvation in Jesus been a source of soul rest?

Matthew 12:1–32

◤ READ MATTHEW 12:1-32

On a Sabbath day, Jesus was walking with His disciples when they stopped to pluck some grains of wheat to eat. Some nearby Pharisees saw this as a violation of rules against harvesting on the Sabbath, so they immediately confronted them. Jesus responded to their criticism with words that would've offended and angered them.

Review 12:3–5. As experts in the Scriptures, the Pharisees certainly would have read the accounts Jesus referenced here. What point was He trying to make by asking these questions?

When the Pharisees passed judgment, they revealed their misdirected zeal about the law. They were familiar with God's messages through Scripture but missed much of His meaning. Jesus vouched for the innocence of His disciples and asserted His authority over the law, calling Himself the Lord of the Sabbath.

Then Jesus went to the synagogue, where He found Himself in the middle of another Sabbath controversy—and this time, it was likely a setup. There was a man at the synagogue who apparently had a physical need, but instead of showing him care and concern, the Pharisees used it as an opportunity to try to trap Jesus. They asked Jesus's opinion about healing on the day of rest, and Jesus—as He often did—started His response with a question.

He pointed out that none of them would think twice about helping their hurt or endangered animal on the Sabbath—the law even made provision for that. Because people made in God's image are even more important than animals, any law keeper should be able to discern that healing on the Sabbath is a way to honor God and come into alignment with His values, not rebel against Him. Again, Jesus pointed out that their stringent, man-made systems undermined God's heart of mercy toward people in need.

Demonstrating the power and compassion the religious leaders lacked, Jesus healed the man. His actions both upheld the law and honored the Father, yet the Pharisees responded by plotting to destroy Him. Jesus was claiming His throne through His works and His words, but the Pharisees saw their kingdom of tradition and control begin to topple.

Even as we follow Jesus, we can hold Pharisaical attitudes in our hearts and minds toward others. Examine your heart. Have you ever found yourself being critical of other Christians based on your own religious traditions or personal convictions?

Now consider the question from the other angle: Are there areas where you don't share the traditions or convictions of other Christians that could be a source of their criticism toward you?

Jesus knew the Pharisees were plotting to put Him to death, and that it would eventually come to pass according to the Father's plan, but He also knew it wasn't the proper time yet. He moved on from that place, not out of fear of the Pharisees but to continue fulfilling the Father's plan.

Many people followed Jesus as He resumed restoring health and setting people free. No issue or affliction was a match for His authority—blindness, muteness, demon-oppression—He was King over it all.

Review 12:22–24. Compare and contrast how "the people" and the Pharisees responded to the miracle Jesus performed.

The People	The Pharisees

Jesus wasted no time calling out the wild claims of the Pharisees. He confronted what came out of their mouths and even their secret thoughts. He said the whole foundation of their argument was flawed—a divided kingdom was a nonsensical strategy. Even though He knew they wouldn't accept it, He clearly communicated the truth: He was casting out the spirit of Satan by the Spirit of God. What they had tried to discredit was divine power on display—the kingdom of God had come upon them.

Jesus wasn't shrinking back or shying away from statements He knew would cause a stir. He declared a clear division between Satan's kingdom of darkness and His kingdom of light with no potential for neutral parties. As rightful Ruler, He laid out the rules—people were either exclusively allegiant to Him or against Him.

Using your favorite commentary, summarize your understanding of "blasphemy against the Holy Spirit."

In calling Jesus an agent of Beelzebub, the Pharisees were attributing God's work to Satan. Jesus said this type of sin was in a category of its own: blasphemy of the Holy Spirit. In maligning Jesus—and specifically the source of His power—they spoke slanderously about the Holy Spirit in a unique way. What the Pharisees were doing wasn't fueled by ignorant unbelief but willful opposition. They knew that what they were asserting about Jesus's miracles wasn't true, but they were unwilling to acknowledge it, and He warned them of the eternal implications of that choice.

Review 12:31–32. What is your initial reaction to Jesus's statement that there is a sin that will not be forgiven? What seems to be the difference between "every sin and blasphemy" that is forgivable and "blasphemy against the Spirit"?

Jesus wasn't trying to cause panic around the possibility of committing the "unpardonable sin." (And in fact, many believe this sin isn't possible today since Jesus is no longer walking the earth as God-man.) He warned those who were walking on that path of where it led. While those who consciously resist and refuse Jesus will ultimately be rejected, He will never condemn the one who comes to Him in repentance and faith.

Matthew 12:33–50

READ MATTHEW 12:33–50

By this point in Jesus's ministry, there was plenty of proof circulating that He was the promised King. Miracles here, authoritative teachings there, and fulfilled prophecies everywhere. Yet in 12:38 some scribes and Pharisees asked Jesus to show them a sign—as if there were insufficient evidence. Today, we have even more evidence to support the case that Jesus is who He said He was, but we see the same rejection and dismissal.

What things do people commonly say they'd have to know or experience in order to believe in Jesus or surrender to Him?

Jesus was in no way at a loss for words after the Pharisees' blasphemous accusations. He called them a brood of vipers—they had shown their true colors with their response to His most recent miracle. Just like trees bearing good or bad fruits indicate their respective good or bad health, evil or righteous words reveal the status of the hearts they flow out of. Our words have weight; they matter. While Jesus was specifically addressing the Pharisees here, He was also offering a general truth about the importance of speaking with intention and integrity.

Use your Bible or an online Bible to look up each of the cross-references for Matthew 12:36–37. How do the verses contribute to your understanding of what Jesus is saying about judgment and what constitutes careless words?

Since the religious leaders appeared to be losing their verbal altercation with Jesus, they shifted gears and asked Him to demonstrate His power. On the surface, their request sounded sincere, but His response gave a glimpse into what was happening in their hearts.

Review 12:39. What two words does Jesus use to describe the types of people who seek a sign?

_____

_____

Jesus didn't give them the sign they were looking for, but He said they'd be privy to the only sign they'd ever need to see: the sign of Jonah—meaning He would spend three days and three nights in the grave after His death on the cross.

Even the people of wicked Nineveh would condemn these religious leaders for their lack of belief in Jesus. The Ninevites responded with repentance to the message of Jonah the prophet (Jonah 3:5). Likewise, the Queen of Sheba listened to and praised the wisdom of Solomon, who was the wisest man to ever live (1 Kings 4:29–34, 10:6–9). But Someone even greater than Solomon was speaking to them, and they weren't humble enough to receive it.

Jesus knew that regardless of any signs He showed them, they wouldn't believe because they were spiritually blind. He made it clear that this evil and adulterous generation had a bleak future ahead. They were like a person repossessed by a demon who returned with a squad of even more sinister friends because it realized it had found a safe place to set up base. Jesus was giving them a warning. In their resistance to His divine authority as King—leaving the homes of their hearts unoccupied—the people had made themselves even more susceptible to forces of the kingdom of darkness who could come to take up residence.

Mid-conversation, Jesus's family showed up, hoping to get a word with Him. He had been drawing attention for going toe-to-toe with the religious head honchos of the day, and His family was likely worried about Him. When a man went to relay the message to Jesus that His mom and brothers were waiting outside, that guy and the surrounding crowd ended up getting a message of their own.

Using your favorite Bible commentary, look up 12:46–50. Why would it be wrong to interpret this as a declaration that biological family is unimportant? What point was Jesus trying to make through this statement?

How might the way you relate to your church (local body of believers) and the Church (all believers) change if Jesus's emphasis on spiritual family became more of your reality?

Jesus was expanding their idea of what family is, emphasizing the greater significance of the bond of the family of God. While earthly and biological family brings a temporary bond, the bond of the family of God is an eternal one. Jesus called people to Himself and invited them to be part of this eternal family. He knew this would be a cherished gift for many who would follow Him at the cost of having their biological siblings, parents, and children turn against them (Matthew 10:21–22, 10:36).

The family Jesus was bringing together would be better than the most wonderful earthly ones, and it would be redemptive even for the most desperately broken ones. His is a kingdom family unified around a merciful and righteous King!

Matthew 13:1–33

READ MATHEW 13:1-33

Jesus was really good at gathering a crowd. We repeatedly see that when Jesus was speaking, people showed up. All-in followers, apprehensive seekers, and staunch skeptics alike came from near and far to hear the Man who spoke with amazing authority, often using parables.

Using a Bible commentary for help, summarize what a parable is and describe its purpose.

This oratory approach wasn't Jesus randomly trying something new. It was an intentional turning point in His ministry, marking a new movement in the concerto of the King that would soon reach its crescendo at the cross. Parables are simple stories, usually containing only a few unnamed characters, that illustrate one primary point. It can be tempting to try to break down every element of these stories to extract deeper meaning—and sometimes that can be helpful—but it's important to remember that most parables are only intended to make one complex issue clearer.

Jesus started His string of seven parables with a story about seeds sown on different soils and what happens in each situation. After He finished the first parable of the series, the disciples called for a time-out to ask Jesus why He was speaking in coded language.

What does the disciples' coming to Jesus with a question show about their relationship with Him? What does it reveal about their relationship with His teaching?

When God says or does something in Scripture or in your life that is hard to understand or hear, is your instinct to take your questions to Him? Why or why not?

Look up the verses below and write out the one(s) that encourage or challenge you most:

James 1:5–8 _____

Psalm 73:16–17 _____

Psalm 119:130 _____

John 14:26 _____

The disciples weren't afraid to ask Jesus about things they didn't understand. Jesus is an approachable and accessible King, so He took an intermission to provide some perspective.

His coded language was intentional, He said. The secrets of the king-dom had been *given* to the disciples. But to others—the audience at large—those secrets had not been revealed. Jesus makes a distinction between His disciples and the crowds.

Review 13:13–17. What differences between the two groups does He describe?

Jesus didn't say the disciples were *better* than those who didn't understand His teachings about the kingdom of God—He said they were *blessed*. They had been given a gift, through no effort or merit of their own. People can have functioning eyes, ears, and minds in a physical sense, but still not be able to perceive the kingdom.

Read 1 Corinthians 2:14. What does the text say about the ability to understand spiritual things? What is necessary to understand the truth?

While the truth is hidden from some, Scripture says those who seek will find (Matthew 7:7). Jesus is not in the business of rejecting those who come to Him compelled by genuine desire and curiosity. The religious leaders tried to trap, trick, and accuse Him, but He repeatedly welcomed those who brought Him their questions and doubts.

Review 13:18–23. Fill in the chart below with the details about each type of soil.

Soil Type	Verse(s)	What thwarts or helps the seed?	What is the result?

In His next three parables, Jesus talked about weeds, more seeds, and a little bit of leaven. These particular parables revealed what the kingdom of heaven looks like as it grows. In the first, He used the image of weeds growing alongside grain to represent evil and corruption that would show up in the midst of the good kingdom. God would sort things out, but it would happen eventually, not immediately.

In the second parable, Jesus used the visual of a tiny mustard seed growing into a large, looming tree to illustrate how His kingdom—one with seemingly small beginnings—would advance and grow into something that far exceeded expectations and imaginations. It would be a nest of rest and refuge for *all* nations!

His final parable used leaven in what appears to be a positive way. In the same way a little bit of leaven impacts everything it touches, so will the kingdom of heaven. Jesus and His kingdom are an unstoppable force, and those in the kingdom will leave their mark on the world around them!

Matthew 13:34–58

READ MATTHEW 13:34–58

In today's passage, Matthew was doing one of his favorite things—connecting the dots between Jesus and the Jewish Scriptures. Every time Matthew referenced Jesus fulfilling prophecy, he wasn't just listing fun facts—he was providing proof that Jesus is the promised King.

In light of the themes Jesus was addressing in His parables, what is the relevance of establishing that Jesus is the King?

As He continued to share parables, Jesus clarified more kingdom realities. But this time He did it in a more intimate setting, where He spoke directly to His disciples. His audience was all ears. He backtracked to break down the parable of the weeds (per the disciples' request). Then He unpacked two more parables: a hidden treasure and precious pearl.

Review 13:44–46. With the King's heart and kingdom values in mind, what point do you see Jesus making in the parable of the hidden treasure? In the parable of the precious pearl?

Hidden Treasure	
Precious Pearl	

Remember every parable has one primary, overarching point. Don't get stuck in the weeds trying to decipher every detail. You're not trying to solve a puzzle—you're trying to see the principle.

Using your favorite Bible commentary, look up 13:44–50 and note anything new you notice or learn.

There are a few widely accepted interpretations of these parables, many of which put the emphasis on *us*. But in light of His theme of revealing the kingdom and His heart as King, it seems likely that the parable would be centered on *Him*. Jesus is the King who would pay the ultimate price to possess what He treasured—the thing that brought Him deep joy.

Read Isaiah 53. Take note of any places you see the theme(s) of these two parables at play.

His last parable is reminiscent of the parable of the weeds (13:36–43), except using fishing imagery. Since Peter, Andrew, James, and John had left their nets to follow Jesus, they likely would've connected deeply with the illustration. Just as a skilled fisherman would use a dragnet to scoop up everything in his path and sort it out after it was pulled into the boat, the angels at the end of the age would separate the evil and the righteous.

Given that not everyone could grasp Jesus's teachings, He asked His disciples if they understood Him. When they confirmed that they did, He used an analogy to encourage them. The new things they were learning from Him should be treasured alongside the things they'd already learned from the Scriptures. Both were valuable and worth holding on to in the treasury of their relationship with God.

What true things did you know about God before becoming a Christian or reading the Bible for yourself?

What truths have you heard or learned about God since becoming a Christian or reading the Bible that have expanded the treasury of your relationship with Him?

After His discussion with the disciples, Jesus packed up, headed to His hometown, and did more teaching in the synagogue. The locals were impressed at first, but after they rejected Him, He didn't do many miracles.

Are there areas of doubt in your life? What doubts might you need to repent of today?

God knows your heart—and that should be a comforting thought. None of your doubts or fears are a surprise to Him. He invites His kids to talk to Him openly about the things we struggle with. If this week's lessons and parables have left you frustrated or confused, take some time to tell Him about it and to dig deeper as you try to get to know Him more. In His expansive kingdom, you are one of the treasures the King takes delight in. Draw near to Him today—because He's where the joy is!

What stood out to you most in this week's study? Why?

What did you learn or relearn about God and His character this week?

Corresponding Psalm & Prayer

 READ PSALM 84

What correlation do you see between Psalm 84 and this week's study of Jesus and His kingdom?

What portions stand out to you most?

Close by praying this prayer aloud:

> *Father,*
> *Your kingdom is beautiful! In it all things are set right. You are on the throne, and You can be trusted, even in the darkest times.*
> *Father, I have sinned, and I appeal to Your mercy. I confess that I have doubted Your fairness and goodness. Like John the Baptist,*

my circumstances have prompted me to despair at times. I've mistrusted Your heart, thinking You're withholding something good from me. I repent of my sins and turn to You and ask You to make my heart clean.

Grant me ears to hear You, eyes to see You, and a heart that loves You more as I get to know You more. Grant me trust in You, that I might believe the new things You reveal to me about Yourself.

I surrender my life to You, Lord—every moment of my day, each decision I make, I yield my will and way to Your perfect will and way.

I love You too. Amen.

Rest, Catch Up, or Dig Deeper

 WEEKLY CHALLENGE

Jesus said, "Come to me, all who labor and are heavy laden, and I will give you rest. Take my yoke upon you, and learn from me, for I am gentle and lowly in heart, and you will find rest for your souls. For my yoke is easy, and my burden is light" (Matthew 11:28–30).

When you feel worn out, burdened, anxious, or overwhelmed, where do you turn? Jesus calls us to come to Him to find a rest that goes beyond our bodies and minds—He wants rest for our *souls*.

In an eternal sense, when we repent and believe in Him we're responding to His invitation to find our eternal rest in Him. But His invitation applies to our everyday lives as well. He is our best choice for refreshment and strength in the face of false or superficial rests.

Write out Matthew 11:28–30 in your journal at the top of a blank page. Throughout the week, write down the things you find yourself reflexively running toward when you need rest. (You might even be able to identify some of them in advance. If so, go ahead and write them down now.) If those things aren't Jesus, ask Him to search your heart and reveal these things to you: Why do you run to those things, how has that choice impacted you in the past, and what might help you lean into His offer to give your soul rest?

Matthew 14–16:
Purpose of the King

DAILY BIBLE READING

Day 1: Matthew 14
Day 2: Matthew 15:1–20
Day 3: Matthew 15:21–39
Day 4: Matthew 16:1–20
Day 5: Matthew 16:21–28
Day 6: Psalm 34
Day 7: Catch-Up Day

Corresponds to Days 290 and 292–293 of *The Bible Recap*.

WEEKLY CHALLENGE

See page 129 for more information.

Matthew 14

READ MATTHEW 14

After being manipulated by his wife and stepdaughter, Herod Antipas had John the Baptist (JTB) beheaded in prison. The Israelites likely would've interpreted this as a political, religious, or moral attack. After all, one of their leaders was killed for telling the truth.

What truth did John the Baptist tell that led to his murder?

After JTB's disciples respectfully buried what remained of his body, they went to tell Jesus what had happened. They took their anger, grief, and disbelief—brought on by the evil actions of a powerful political ruler—to Jesus. And as Jesus and His disciples retreated to process their own grief together, a crowd began to assemble. Word had spread that the Roman-appointed ruler of their region had murdered one of their leaders. And God's people, carrying their own emotional baggage of despair and fear, came in droves to find Jesus, the good King.

How did the disciples respond to the great crowd of people?

How did Jesus respond to His disciples?

Jesus, who is fully God and fully man, provides for both souls and bodies. In John's account of the same story, we learn that the crowd Jesus just fed wanted to make Him the Roman king (John 6:15). While they believed in His power and had experienced His goodness, they didn't yet understand His divinity. Jesus didn't intend to be king of the Israelites or even king of the powerful Roman empire. He came as *the* King—the King over all kings.

How did the people's view of a king differ from Jesus's true role as King?

The People's Expectation	Jesus as King

As Jesus spent time by Himself praying, His disciples were out on the Sea of Galilee. Several of them were experienced fishermen, but they had been battling a rough storm for about nine hours, and it had pushed them three miles out to sea. They were mourning the death of JTB, exhausted from feeding thousands, and weary from battling the storm. On top of that, they thought they saw a ghost approaching them! When Jesus revealed that it wasn't a ghost but Him, He calmed their fears using some of the same language God used when He identified Himself to Moses in the Old Testament.

Read Exodus 3. What is the context of Exodus 3:14? Why did Jesus use similar language with His disciples during the storm?

Though it may chafe against our love for miracles and wonders, the high point of this scene isn't Peter walking on water or Jesus quieting the winds and the waves. The high point is the worship of the King and the acknowledgment that He is the Son of God. Walking on water happened *once*, but Jesus is King *eternally*!

We see this repeatedly throughout Jesus's ministry. At the end of chapter 14, Matthew said that even in a town where Jesus hadn't traveled before, the people *recognized* Him and brought Him everyone who was sick. They begged Jesus to let the sick touch the hem of His clothes, and those who did were made well. They believed they would be healed—not because their faith was strong, but because Jesus is unmatched in power and love. The strength of our faith matters, but the object of our faith matters infinitely more.

How does our society today focus on the *strength* of a person's faith?

How can you push back against those messages and focus on the *object* of your faith?

Matthew 15:1–20

 READ MATTHEW 15:1–20

Once again, the Pharisees attempted to catch Jesus and His disciples breaking Jewish law. These religious leaders traveled from Jerusalem to Galilee—a trip of nearly eighty miles that likely would've taken eight days—to pose their question: Why didn't Jesus's disciples wash their hands before eating? At the time, this wasn't a hygienic practice, but one of rabbinical ceremony and tradition. In other words, this wasn't one of God's rules—this was one of *their* rules. Jesus answered them by calling out their hypocrisy—they were breaking one of God's rules in the way they treated their fathers and mothers.

What prophecy from Isaiah did Jesus say pointed to the Pharisees?

Jesus went on to say that it's not what goes into the mouth that defiles someone, but what comes out. It would be difficult to overstate how confusing this was for His Jewish disciples. In their minds, Jesus was contradicting everything they grew up learning about the law. Peter even assumed that Jesus was telling one of His parables! But remember Jesus's words from Matthew 5:17: "Do not think that I have come to abolish the Law or the Prophets; I have not come to abolish them but to fulfill them."

Read Leviticus 11. What are some of the laws concerning animals that the disciples would've followed their whole lives?

After this encounter, Jesus gave a brief commentary on the Pharisees. He told His disciples that while the Pharisees may have had the appearance of being God's kids, they weren't. And everyone who wasn't in God's family would eventually be rooted up. By adding to God's laws, the Pharisees, who were the religious leaders of the people, misled others down that path too. When a leader can't see clearly, both they and their followers end up in a pit.

It's important to remember that Jesus wasn't disregarding God's law here; He was denouncing the religious traditions these men added to God's law. Jesus didn't come to get rid of the law, replace the law, or ignore the law. Since He came to fulfill the law, the law must be interpreted through Him. In ways that were more radical than the disciples could understand at the time, His life and teachings show us how to understand the Old Testament. The whole of the Old Testament—the law and the prophets—points to Him, the King, the sacrificial Messiah (Luke 24:25–27, 44–45; John 5:39–40, 46). Jesus emphasized His proclamation again in verse 20 as only the perfect, law-fulfilling King could: "To eat with unwashed hands does not defile anyone."

Review 15:18–20. What things did Jesus say can defile a person?

_____

_____

_____

_____

_____

_____

_____

How have you seen the things listed above defile a person? How have you seen them defile you? **(Look up the definition of *defile* in a dictionary to help you reflect.)**

Ceremonial laws of the Old Testament reminded the Israelites that their sin was a barrier to a full, thriving relationship with God. The only person to have ever kept the entire law perfectly was Jesus. As a result, He is the only one who can forgive our sin and remove the barrier between us and God. He fulfilled the law, paid the price for our sins, and restored us to a right relationship with God the Father. Because of His sinless life, faithful death, and miraculous resurrection, we are justified through Him and reconciled to the Father. Praise Christ! He did what we could never do!

Matthew 15:21–39

◤◥ READ MATTHEW 15:21–39

In yesterday's reading, the Pharisees took a long road trip, motivated by an issue that seemed insignificant. And in today's reading, Jesus and His disciples took a long road trip as well. It's interesting to think about what may have prompted His travels.

Jesus withdrew to a coastal area about forty miles north of His hometown. The district of Tyre and Sidon was a curious place to "withdraw" because it was outside of Jewish territory. In Gentile regions, Jesus could speak freely about what He had to offer the people, because He didn't have to worry about them trying to make Him their king. The Gentiles weren't expecting a King like the Jews were.

And of course, He knew who would be there looking for Him. A Canaanite woman, a desperate mother with a demonized daughter in need of healing, begged for an audience with Jesus—so fervently, in fact, that the disciples even asked Jesus to send her away.

She called Jesus "Lord, Son of David." While she used the simple version of the word *Lord* to show honor, not to acknowledge His lordship, her use of *Son of David* carried a bit more weight. It seems to indicate that she had picked up some clues about His identity. Even though she was a Gentile, she had heard of His miracles and believed in His power.

When she asked Him to heal her daughter, Jesus told her that He was sent for the lost sheep of the house of Israel, meaning the Jews. Up until this point in His ministry, His focus was on the Jewish people and their spiritual needs. The woman knew this and humbled herself, kneeling in front of Him and asking again for His help.

Jesus responded to her in a way that the people of the time would've understood: by turning an insult used for Gentiles into an affectionate play on words: "It is not right to take the children's bread and throw it to the dogs" (15:26). The common word Jews used to refer to Gentiles, *kuon*, referred to an unclean animal. But Jesus's word was *kunarion*, the term for a pet dog, and it carries the connotation of a term of endearment.

Her response is extraordinary. She didn't claim to have a right to the blessings God promised to Israel. She didn't demand an exception to God's covenant with Israel. And she didn't argue that Jesus was being unfair. Rather, she humbly asked for crumbs: "Yes, Lord, yet even the dogs eat the crumbs that fall from their masters' table" (15:27).

Read Genesis 12:3. As a Gentile, what promise was the Canaanite woman counting on? How does that promise apply to us today?

Jesus praised the woman's faith and healed her daughter. It's worth noting that nothing else is mentioned on this trip. It seems that perhaps the whole road trip was for this woman and her daughter—much like the trip to the Gadarenes to heal the two demonized men in that Gentile region.

After this, Jesus headed back to the hills around the Sea of Galilee. More people came to Him—thousands of them. And according to most commentators, the audience in this region was almost certainly filled with Gentiles. They brought the sick, wounded, and disabled to Him, and He healed them.

Review 15:31. How did the (likely Gentile) crowd respond to Jesus's healings?

For *three days*, Jesus healed the people in this region. And again, we see that Jesus wasn't concerned only for their souls, but their bodies as well. A familiar scene unfolded: Jesus told His disciples that He didn't want to send the people away without anything to eat.

What did the disciples ask Jesus in verse 33? What does this tell us about them?

Just as He did in Matthew 14, Jesus took a small amount of food, gave thanks to the Father, broke the bread, and had His disciples distribute the food. Just as before, there was more than enough for everyone. Earlier, when Jesus fed the five thousand, there were twelve baskets left over, likely symbolizing His care for the twelve disciples. This time, however, there were seven baskets left over. In Judaism, the number seven symbolizes completion or perfection. Here, we see the abundance of Jesus's kingdom that extends beyond Jews to include Gentiles. Completion. Perfection.

In these Gentile territories, Jesus extended Himself with great patience and compassion, healing the sick and providing for the poor. His kingdom is for everyone, and in His kingdom, even the crumbs are abundant!

How have you seen God's abundance in your life?

Matthew 16:1–20

READ MATTHEW 16:1-20

Nothing unites broken people like a common enemy, and that's how chapter sixteen opens. No sooner had Jesus returned from ministry in the Gentile land than the Pharisees and the Sadducees, who usually despised each other, joined forces to try to trick Him.

They asked Him—the Messiah—for a sign about . . . the Messiah. So Jesus put them in their place pretty quickly and responded in a way that today would sound something like this: "Anyone who sees dark clouds and smells rain knows to grab an umbrella."

Review Matthew 13:33 and 16:5–12. What is the difference between the analogies Jesus used for leaven?

After Jesus clarified to His disciples that He was speaking figuratively (so they needed to stop talking about bread already!), they understood His message: Even a small amount of sin has a huge impact. In Jesus's time, Pharisees were often hypocritical, while Sadducees were skeptical. They both had areas of their religious lives that were out of alignment with God's ways, which led them further astray.

How have you seen small amounts of hypocrisy and/or skepticism have a large impact?

More than any other name Jesus used to refer to Himself, He said He is the Son of Man. In Daniel 7, the Son of Man—someone who is both human and divine—is given power, glory, and a kingdom. Here in Matthew, Jesus asked His disciples who people were saying the Son of Man was. It's important to note that no group was openly confessing Jesus as the Messiah at that time. Some of His followers had glimpses of who He was, but none had the full picture yet.

As he often did, Peter answered Jesus on behalf of the disciples. Who did Peter say that Jesus was?

Jesus told Peter that only God could have given him so full an understanding of who Jesus is. Jesus then told Peter (whose name *petros* means "pebble" in Greek) that His Church would be built on this rock (*petra* or "mountain" in Greek). The rock that the Church would be built on isn't Peter. It can't be; Peter is a pebble. The mountain-rock that the Church would be built on was the truth that Peter confessed: "You are the Christ, the Son of the living God" (16:16).

Look up Acts 4:11. According to Peter, who is the cornerstone of the Church?

Look up 1 Corinthians 3:11. According to Paul, who is the foundation of the Church?

In stone masonry, the cornerstone and the foundation stone are the same piece—the most important piece in a structure. If this stone were to be removed, the whole building would collapse. While Jesus affirmed Peter's statement of faith, this moment really wasn't about Peter at all—it was about King Jesus the Messiah, the Son of Man, the foundation of our faith.

This is also the first mention in the Bible of the Church. In Acts, we read about the day of Pentecost, when the Holy Spirit descended and the Church was formed (Acts 2). The Church is made up of all believers—both Jewish and Gentile—and anything it does within God's will bears His name. In this passage, Jesus spoke to Peter as a member of the disciples and as a member of all believers to come, and He said that even death won't kill His Church! This would be an important reminder to His disciples in the days to come, as the early church would face incredible persecution.

Review 16:20. Why would Jesus tell the disciples that they couldn't tell anyone that He was the Christ? Refer back to Day 1 of Week 3 (page 65), where we discussed the messianic secret. Write out any thoughts or questions you have about what it would have been like for the disciples to live in this tension.

Matthew 16:21–28

 READ MATTHEW 16:21–28

What does 16:21 say Jesus began to show His disciples?

The disciples' confession of faith would soon be followed by Jesus's journey to Jerusalem and the cross. Jesus, fully God and fully man, came not as a prophet or a healer or a moral teacher. Jesus the King came to suffer and to sacrifice Himself for our sins. He reconciled us to God so that we as believers could join Him in His everlasting kingdom as heirs. *This* is the purpose of the King.

How did Peter respond to Jesus once He revealed His purpose? **Review Matthew 4:1–11.** What similarities do you notice?

When Peter rebuked Jesus, Jesus strongly corrected him, saying "Get behind me, Satan!" Even though Peter had just made a profound profession of faith, he was still fully human, with a limited understanding of God's plan for our redemption. In Matthew 4, Satan tempted Jesus to take the glory of being King without the suffering of being Savior. But Jesus knew that without His suffering, there could be no salvation. Without death, there is no resurrection. Without the cross, there is no Christianity. And without the shedding of His blood, there could be no forgiveness of our sins (Hebrews 9:22). His death was necessary.

What three things did Jesus instruct His disciples to do in 16:24?

_____

_____

_____

The way to the glorious kingdom is the cross. The instructions to us today are the same as they were to His disciples. We also must set down our entitlement, embrace His will, and follow wherever He leads. Contrary to the trite way many of us have named minor inconveniences as "our crosses to bear," Jesus instructed His followers to completely submit to God's authority.

In what areas of your life do you hold entitlement? What would submitting completely to God's authority in these areas look like?

Jesus warned of two hindrances to a walk with Him: self-preservation and seeking wealth. Both of these are natural tendencies for humans. Some might even call them lifesaving. But in Jesus's kingdom, you have to lose your life to find it. We must refuse to lean on our own efforts and strength—we must lean fully on the finished work of Christ, trusting God for our salvation and sanctification (1 Peter 3:18, Leviticus 20:7–8). Praise God for the great love He has for us in sending His Son, the King, to show us the way to His kingdom! He's where the joy is!

What stood out to you most in this week's study? Why?

What did you learn or relearn about God and His character this week?

Corresponding Psalm & Prayer

 READ PSALM 34

What correlation do you see between Psalm 34 and this week's study of Jesus and His kingdom?

What portions stand out to you most?

Close by praying this prayer aloud:

> *Father,*
>   *Your heart is so attentive and kind! Every aspect of timing, every word spoken, every detail—You are in it. Thank You for the ways You care for Your kids so well. You show up when our hearts are broken,*

You draw near when we're sick and in need. We see it in the story of Jesus going out of His way to meet with the Canaanite woman and heal her demonized daughter. We see it in His compassion toward the thousands of hungry Gentiles. And I see it in the way You care for me too—and I praise You for it.

Father, I have sinned, and I appeal to Your mercy. I confess that I'm often entitled and demanding. When my expectations go unmet, I sometimes lack patience or humility. I have leaned into self-preservation. Like the Pharisees, I've been hypocritical and legalistic, and like the Sadducees, I've grown cynical in certain areas. I repent of my sins and turn to You and ask You to make my heart clean.

Soften my heart—for Your glory and my joy! Help me to help those You place in my path instead of finding reasons to accuse or dismiss them. Give me eyes to see people the way You see them and love them the way You love them. Give me the wisdom to live with a kingdom mindset, not an earthly mindset.

I surrender my life to You, Lord—every moment of my day, each decision I make, I yield my will and way to Your perfect will and way.

I love You too. Amen.

Rest, Catch Up, or Dig Deeper

 WEEKLY CHALLENGE

Those of us who grew up hearing Bible stories like the ones of Jesus feeding the crowds can tend to put ourselves in the stories. Here, let's think of ourselves not as the child bringing our meager offering and asking Jesus to multiply it. Rather, let's think of ourselves as those who are blessed by God's extravagant abundance. This will serve as a good reminder that it's not what we can do for Him, but what He has done for us.

This week, gather seven cards or pieces of paper. On five of the cards, draw a loaf. On two of the cards, draw a fish. These drawings can be as simple or as creative as you'd like. Inside each of the drawings, write a category of blessing in your life (family, friends, church, home, work, etc.).

Throughout the week, add specific notes to each card as you reflect on God's overflowing goodness in your life in that specific area. Thank Him for the specific gifts He's given you and the ways in which He provides for your soul and your body.

Matthew 17–19:

Perspective of the King

DAILY BIBLE READING

Day 1: Matthew 17

Day 2: Matthew 18:1–14

Day 3: Matthew 18:15–35

Day 4: Matthew 19:1–12

Day 5: Matthew 19:13–30

Day 6: Psalm 131

Day 7: Catch-Up Day

Corresponds to Days 294–295 and 304 of *The Bible Recap*.

WEEKLY CHALLENGE

See page 151 for more information.

Matthew 17

 READ MATTHEW 17

Look up *transfigure* in a dictionary. What does it mean?

Review 17:2. How did Jesus transfigure?

Peter, James, and John were profoundly moved by the awesome sight of the transfiguration and the surprising presence of the other witnesses—Moses and Elijah. Together, those two represented the whole Old Testament (the law and the prophets, respectively), which points in its entirety to Jesus, the Messiah King. Peter, with his rashness on full display, attempted to find a way to stay in that moment longer, but he was quickly humbled when God the Father cut him off mid-speech and revealed Himself.

Read Exodus 13:21–22 and 1 Kings 8:10–11. What do you notice about how God revealed Himself there? **Then review Matthew 17:5.** What did God tell the disciples here?

When Jesus touched the cowering disciples, they looked up and saw only the King. The transfiguration was a picture of His coming glory. Jesus knew the time for revealing His purpose on earth was coming quickly, and with it would come great suffering. He also knew how the disciples would respond to this. In fact, a few verses later, Jesus told the disciples again of His death and resurrection, and "they were greatly distressed" (17:23).

When Jesus spoke of His death, He also spoke of His resurrection. But the disciples, who only understood a portion of Jesus's identity and not His full divinity, heard this and focused exclusively on the part pertaining to His death. So in the transfiguration, Jesus gave His closest disciples a glimpse of the full picture: The King came down and humbled Himself to suffer, *and the King will come again in His full glory.*

Jesus also knew that the time for His purpose was coming soon, but it wasn't there yet. So He told the three disciples: "Tell no one the vision, until the Son of Man is raised from the dead" (17:9).

Read Malachi 4:5, then review Matthew 17:10–13. What did Jesus clarify for the disciples? Why is this important?

When Jesus returned to the rest of His disciples and a crowd, He healed a demon-possessed boy who His disciples could not. When they asked why they couldn't heal him, Jesus pointed out their lack of faith. He told them that faith as small as a mustard seed can move a mountain. This verse is often misquoted and misclaimed. Remember that Jesus had given His disciples ability and authority to cast out demons and to heal in His name. Rightly directed action with rightly placed faith can do things that are otherwise impossible.

How have you heard Matthew 17:20 taken out of context? What does it really mean? What does that look like today?

Matthew 17 ends with a story about taxes that is only recorded by Matthew, the former tax collector. How fitting! Since Moses's time, each Israelite over the age of twenty had to pay two drachmas, or half a shekel, to support the tabernacle. Fifteen hundred years later, the same rule still applied for supporting the temple. The Pharisees came to ask Peter why Jesus had failed to pay His taxes. From everything we know, Jesus didn't carry money. But He ensured the temple tax was paid for Himself and for Peter—who may not have even been old enough to owe the tax—through a miracle.

How did the temple tax get paid? How was this a miracle?

Jesus told Peter that even though the sons of earthly kings don't pay taxes for the king's home, He would pay the temple tax to avoid offense. Later in the New Testament, Paul echoed Jesus's intentions here: "For though I am free from all, I have made myself a servant to all, that I might win more of them" (1 Corinthians 9:19). Our gracious King modeled for us how to focus on the heart of the gospel, removing barriers to reach more people.

Are there barriers in your life that might prevent others from seeing God and His love more clearly? Ask God to search your heart and reveal anything in your life that you might want to adjust to be kingdom minded instead of earthly minded.

Matthew 18:1–14

READ MATTHEW 18:1-14

Beginning in chapter 18, Jesus painted a picture of His kingdom, answering questions about what the kingdom looks like and how it should be known. The disciples came to Him with a jarringly self-seeking question: "Who is the greatest in the kingdom of heaven?" But before we point fingers and scoff at the disciples' pride, let's reflect on ourselves.

How have you equated your actions with either your salvation or your level of "greatness" in God's eyes? What blessings have you expected from God in exchange for your obedience?

Jesus had a child come and stand in the middle of them, then told His disciples that only those who become like children will enter the kingdom. The child didn't represent innocence or purity, but humility. A young child rarely has long-lasting delusions of self-sufficiency or grandeur. A toddler's insistent "I do it by myself" is quickly followed by cries of frustration and "Help me." Children are wholly dependent on their caregivers to function. Jesus wasn't telling His disciples that they wouldn't join Him in the kingdom—He was pointing out that their hope was in themselves, the toddlers, instead of in their caregiver, the King.

What warnings did Jesus give the disciples about causing a fellow Christ-follower to sin? Complete the table below.

Verse	If . . .	Then . . .
Matthew 18:6	you cause a believer to sin	
Matthew 18:8		cut it off and throw it away.
Matthew 18:9	your eye causes you to sin	

Do these warnings seem to be a bit much? Sin is serious. Sin leads to death. And sin requires a deathly serious solution. Jesus, who is Himself our solution, deliberately used strong language to reiterate this point: *Do not be the reason another believer is led to sin.* Temptations to sin will come in this life, but the one who brings those temptations to fellow believers brings judgment upon himself. This isn't to say we're responsible for the sins of others—that responsibility lies with each individual person—but we're responsible for considering others in our actions. None of us lives only unto ourselves. Our actions impact others, and it's wise, humble, and kind to take that into account.

What sin in your life might also be causing a brother or sister to sin? List some possibilities below. Then read through your list and humbly seek God's grace, freely given to us through Jesus, and ask Him to restore you to His kingdom's ways.

As Jesus teaches about His kingdom, we get a picture of a sheep who's left the herd. The shepherd leaves his flock to find the one who got lost, turned away, or couldn't keep up. The shepherd cares not only for the entire flock of sheep, but for each sheep in the flock.

Read Psalm 100:3 and Revelation 7:17. Then review Matthew 18:10–14. How is Jesus our shepherd?

When Jesus, the Shepherd King, leaves the other ninety-nine to care for the one, He's not abandoning the rest of the sheep. Rather, by caring for the one, He's ensuring that the flock stays whole. Jesus sees His whole kingdom: the flock and the sheep, the forest and the trees, the Church and the believers. Every detail matters to the King!

Matthew 18:15–35

 READ MATTHEW 18:15-35

Jesus continued to paint a picture of His kingdom in today's passage, answering questions about what the kingdom looks like and how it should be known. So after He explained how to respond to our own sin, He told His disciples how to confront a fellow believer who sins against them.

What are the four steps Jesus outlined in this process of righteous confrontation?

Step One

Step Two

Step Three

Step Four

These are a gift to believers as we walk through life together, and they'll apply in many situations where one brother or sister sins against another. As you learn to forgive the way God instructs, you'll have opportunities to practice the steps Jesus listed in this chapter—likely from both sides of the coin, the sinner and the one sinned against. And using the wisdom God gives, you'll also learn when to seek help from a trusted leader to offer forgiveness.

In Jewish culture at the time, forgiving someone three times was considered generous. So Peter probably thought that offering to forgive someone seven times was extravagant. But Jesus taught that forgiveness should be infinite.

He compared His kingdom to an earthly king "who wished to settle accounts." He contacted a servant who owed him a great debt—one so hefty the servant couldn't possibly repay it. His life's earnings would only be a fraction of the massive amount he owed.

What did the king do for his servant? What did that servant do?

Each of us is the unforgiving servant. We will be—and have been—forgiven infinitely more than we will forgive. When we take into account the depth and width of God's forgiveness for each of us, we should be moved to offer others true forgiveness.

There will also be times when you are ready to offer forgiveness, but the person who has sinned against you is unrepentant. In these cases, we follow the steps Jesus gave and maintain a willingness to forgive in our hearts. Because true forgiveness comes from the heart, its impacts are also felt there first. Whether the brother or sister ever acknowledges their sin toward you, your willingness to extend mercy will protect you from developing a bitter spirit.

Later in Scripture, Paul revisited this teaching in his letter to the churches in Ephesus.

Read Ephesians 4:31–32. What instructions did Paul give for kingdom living?

Jesus's kingdom is a place where the last are first, the poor are rich, and the humble are praised. His kingdom should be recognized by its servants, who are harsh with our own sins, gentle with our brothers and sisters, and lavish in our forgiveness—giving what we have received from our generous King!

Matthew 19:1–12

READ MATTHEW 19:1–12

Before we begin, it's important to acknowledge that today's reading is difficult. If feelings of confusion or frustration come up, take them to the Lord. If feelings of shame or condemnation come up, ask God to silence the enemy's lies and replace them with His truth. Romans 8:1 says there is "no condemnation for those who are in Christ Jesus." God can be trusted with our doubts, our struggles, and our sins. He is personal, relational, and sovereign—with all, through all, and over all. Pray and ask God to show you His heart in what Jesus taught here.

Read Matthew 19:1–12. What are your initial thoughts? Feelings? Questions?

When Jesus concluded His ministry in Galilee, He began traveling south to Jerusalem. When the Pharisees heard where He was, they showed up *again* to try and trick Him *again*. Remember that the Pharisees prided themselves on keeping God's law, but they were hypocrites. They often added extra rules on top of God's laws that made their "obedience" extremely visible while simultaneously creating loopholes around the laws of God that were inconvenient to them.

What did the Pharisees ask Jesus?

The Pharisees knew that no matter what Jesus's answer was, someone would be upset. At that time, some Jewish groups held a very strict view of divorce, and it was not permitted in almost any circumstance. Other Jewish groups held a more liberal view, allowing divorce in some cases and remarriage in others. Sound familiar? Today, different denominations, churches, and faith leaders have different convictions about the Bible's teachings on both divorce and remarriage.

Read Mark 10:2–12. Then review Matthew 19:3–9. What is similar in these passages? What is unique to each passage?

In Matthew 19, Jesus knew His questioners, and He knew their games. Pharisees would often justify their extra rules or loopholes by going as far back as they could in the Scriptures. So Jesus beat them there and went straight back to the garden of Eden. Quoting from Genesis 1:27 and 2:24, Jesus taught that God's original design was for a man and a woman to be united as one, in marriage, as a lifelong commitment.

When the Pharisees protested that Moses made provisions for divorce, Jesus equated the necessity of the provisions with the hardness of our hearts. Divorce and adultery wouldn't be issues if hearts were soft, according to Jesus.

Based on Jesus's teaching, what did the disciples conclude in 19:10?

For the disciples, a life of marriage without divorce or remarriage seemed impossibly hard—harder even than staying single. Jesus told them that those who are called to a life of celibacy and singleness should embrace it.

Along those lines, He gave three examples of eunuchs (people who are incapacitated for marriage and children): those born into it, those forced into it, and those who volunteer for it. But be careful not to infer something that He didn't teach here. If you are single now, God might be calling you to a lifetime of celibacy, or He might not be. He knows your heart and your desires, He knows the future He has planned for you, and He works for the good of His kids.

Jesus didn't say that celibacy is easier than marriage, and He didn't say that marriage is easier than celibacy. There are joys and challenges in both. There are opportunities for sanctification in both. Singleness belongs in the kingdom, and there are kingdom rules to live it faithfully. Marriage belongs in the kingdom, and there are kingdom rules to live it faithfully.

The Pharisees' intention was to set a trap for Jesus by forcing Him into either an unfaithful or uncompassionate mandate about divorce. But Jesus answered them with artistry as the Designer, with compassion as the Savior, and with authority as the King. He spoke beyond what was merely allowed or prohibited in His kingdom. He painted a picture that shows us what His kingdom looks like and how it should be known. Pray that God will teach you how to live faithfully in His kingdom, wherever He's placed you.

If you have any struggles with Jesus's teachings in today's reading, write out a prayer below asking God to meet you in that space with His gentleness, truth, love, and hope.

Matthew 19:13–30

🔺 READ MATTHEW 19:13-30

In most ancient cultures, children were valued not for who they were, but for who they would become. In Israel, the view was somewhat different—children were celebrated as a blessing from God to their families, but they were also expected to remain largely unseen and unheard until they grew up.

How are those cultural beliefs evident in the disciples' reaction to children in verse 13? What did Jesus's response reveal about His kingdom?

After blessing the children, Jesus turned His attention to a rich young man who asked what he needed to do to earn eternal life.

How would you expect Jesus to answer this question?

The man saw salvation as transactional, and not relational. When Jesus told the man to keep the commandments, he had an opportunity to reflect on his failure. No one, except Jesus, had ever kept—or ever will keep—the commandments perfectly. But instead of being convicted of his sin, the man asked Jesus which specific commandments he needed to keep.

Which five commandments did Jesus quote to the man? What do those particular commandments have in common?

When the man insisted that he had followed all of those commandments, Jesus pushed further for a heart examination, telling him, "If you would be perfect, go, sell what you have and give to the poor, and you will have treasure in heaven; and come, follow me" (19:21). At this, the man should have been convicted to realize that his wealth was his god. He should have confessed that he hadn't followed the commandments fully. He should have abandoned his attempts to save himself for Jesus's better way. But all the man heard was an instruction that he was unwilling to follow. So he left in sorrow.

God gives His kids generous gifts, and sometimes these gifts are in the form of material possessions. But brothers and sisters, hear this: If your worldly wealth has become an idol, or if it is creating room in your heart for the lie that you don't need God for every breath you breathe, then give it away. The blessings we hold so tightly now pale in comparison to the blessings in store for those who follow Jesus.

In the ESV, reread the last four words of 19:21. What invitation did Jesus give that the man missed?

This was a rare offer from Jesus, but the man was unwilling. Jesus's disciples were among the few who had heard this invitation before. In Matthew 4, Jesus extended this offer to Peter, James, and John, and in response to His invitation, they left their livelihoods and their families to follow Him. And here in 19:27, Peter pointed out the sacrifices the disciples made in response to Jesus's call. Peter wanted a reassurance of blessing in exchange for what they had left behind. Instead of chastising Peter's rashness—which He could have righteously done—Jesus replied graciously.

Review 19:28–30. What is in store for those who have sacrificed in response to Jesus's call?

Eternal life is a gift, not a reward. We don't earn our salvation or His favor—they are given to us through no effort of our own. But Jesus tells us that whatever is sacrificed for the kingdom will be restored, and whatever is done for God will be honored.

Jesus saw beyond what the rich young man saw, He saw beyond what His disciples saw, and He sees beyond what we see. His perspective is sharper, deeper, and wider. He sees His whole kingdom, and He invites us to join Him there. He's where the joy is!

What stood out to you most in this week's study? Why?

What did you learn or relearn about God and His character this week?

Corresponding Psalm & Prayer

 READ PSALM 131

What correlation do you see between Psalm 131 and this week's study of Jesus and His kingdom?

What portions stand out to you most?

Close by praying this prayer aloud:

> *Father,*
>   *You are holy and righteous, and all Your ways are just. You establish laws that are intended for our highest joy! There is no God like You, who blesses His people with His nearness. Through the finished*

work of Your Son, Jesus, You have already accomplished all that You require of us, and through the power of Your Spirit at work in us, You remind us of who we are, while empowering us to walk in Your ways!

Father, I have sinned, and I appeal to Your mercy. I confess that I often find sin more appealing or natural than obedience. When Your ways seem too restrictive or too hard to understand, I'm tempted to give up. Like the rich young ruler, sometimes I'm distracted by the blessings You've given me and I fail to follow You. Sometimes it feels easier to follow my heart or just ask for forgiveness later. I repent of my sins and turn to You and ask You to make my heart clean.

Grant me childlike humility. Grant me faith in Your power as You work in my life. Grant me wisdom to know and walk in Your ways. And grant me the kind of peace that only comes from being in the kingdom of a good and loving King.

I surrender my life to You, Lord—every moment of my day, each decision I make, I yield my will and way to Your perfect will and way.

I love You too. Amen.

Rest, Catch Up, or Dig Deeper

 WEEKLY CHALLENGE

This week, have a conversation with a child in your life, with their parent's permission. Here are a few guidelines: Don't tell them what to do, and don't make them think about their future (e.g., "What do you want to be when you grow up?"). Value them as the image bearer that they already are. Ask them about their day: what they did and who they saw. Ask them about their lives: what they like and who they spend time with. Ask them about their minds: what they're learning about and what they wonder about. And ask them about their souls: what makes them scared and who makes them feel safe.

Write down what the child tells you. Underline examples of honesty, and circle examples of humility. What can you learn from the child's example?

┌─ Scripture to Memorize ─┐

Therefore do not be anxious, saying, "What shall we eat?" or "What shall we drink?" or "What shall we wear?"

Matthew 6:31

Matthew 20–22:
Tensions of the King

DAILY BIBLE READING

Day 1: Matthew 20:1–16

Day 2: Matthew 20:17–34

Day 3: Matthew 21:1–27

Day 4: Matthew 21:28–46

Day 5: Matthew 22

Day 6: Psalm 118

Day 7: Catch-Up Day

Corresponds to Days 305 and 308 of *The Bible Recap*.

WEEKLY CHALLENGE

See page 177 for more information.

Matthew 20:1–16

READ MATTHEW 20:1–16

King Jesus continued explaining His kingdom by telling another parable. This time, His story involved something well-known in ancient Israel: grapes. You might be thinking, *Grapes? Israel is the land of milk and honey. Since when do grapes matter?!* Grapes were important because they're the source of wine. A good vine keeper knows that to make the best wine, you have to harvest the grapes at just the right time. To achieve this perfect timing, vineyard masters often hired day laborers in addition to the regular staff.

Look up Matthew 9:37–38. What similarities do you see between that passage and this parable?

Read Isaiah 5:1–7, Hosea 10:1, and Jeremiah 2:21. What is Israel called in these passages?

Jesus's message remained consistent: There was a need for more laborers in the field. In both the Old and New Testaments, God referred to His people as a vine or a vineyard.

Use a Bible dictionary or commentary to identify the exact time of day represented by these phrases.

First hour: _____

Third hour: _____

Sixth hour: _____

Ninth hour: _____

Eleventh hour: _____

Time of pay: _____

The first group began working at the earliest hour (six in the morning) and agreed on a fair daily wage of one denarius, but when the master acquired the additional groups of workers, they didn't settle on an exact wage. Perhaps the master had a reputation of being a fair boss, or maybe the laborers were so desperate for work that their exact earnings didn't matter. Whatever the reason, the workers agreed to labor for "whatever is right."

In what order did the foreman call the laborers from the field to receive their wages?

What was the payment for each laborer?

How did the first-hour laborers respond?

Read 1 Corinthians 10:6–10 and Philippians 2:14. What is the result of grumbling?

In what areas of your life are you tempted to complain?

It's common to justify complaining and it's easy to understand why the first-hour workers complained, but there's no room in the upside-down kingdom for this kind of entitlement. God is serious about His laborers not being people who complain. Grumbling and complaining reveal a heart that mistrusts God and His goodness.

At the end of this parable, Jesus made a shocking statement. He claimed authority and ownership over all things, then said, "The last will be first, and the first last." This upends all our striving to advance ourselves and our reputation. It reminds us that comparison is a pointless endeavor in the kingdom—because we're all on the same team, we gain more than we've earned, and we're spared the punishment we deserve. In God's kingdom, His generosity supersedes His justice!

How do these truths shape the way you view the laborers in the field alongside you?

How do these truths shape the way you view God—His actions and His heart?

Matthew 20:17–34

◣ READ MATTHEW 20:17-34

As Jesus and His disciples walked toward Jerusalem, He pulled His disciples aside to tell them specific details of His crucifixion—more secret things they'd eventually be able to shout from the rooftops (10:27). For the third time, Jesus told them what would happen to Him in Jerusalem; but as we'll see later, they didn't understand what He plainly stated.

In your own words, describe what happened in 20:20–28.

The mother of James and John (also known as the sons of Zebedee—their father's name) approached Jesus with an earthly kingdom in mind. She wanted her sons to have VIP status in Jesus's kingdom—the closest seats at the royal table. The other disciples were livid over this audacious request. Perhaps they were jealous that they didn't think of it first. But once again, Jesus reoriented His disciples toward the rules of His kingdom: Those who want to be great have to be servants, and those who want to be first must be slaves.

Admittedly, even these beautiful instructions can mislead us if our hearts are set on self-advancement. We can find ourselves serving in order to be viewed as humble or as a means of gaining respect. We can take Jesus's words as a plan of action instead of a reminder of the kind of heart posture God values.

Have you ever served in order to advance yourself? If so, briefly describe the scenario(s) below.

After Jesus finished delivering the tough news and settling this heated moment among His men, He reminded them that He would be the chief example of what His kingdom looks like—sacrificing His life to serve many.

Then He continued on His long, eight-hour uphill journey from Jericho to Jerusalem—closer to His certain death with every step. Per usual, the crowds followed Him. As two blind men realized who was nearby, they began shouting to get His attention.

Read 2 Samuel 7:12–13, 16. What is the significance of the title "Son of David"?

These two blind beggars didn't have the physical ability to see God, but they had spiritual eyes to recognize the promised Messiah in their midst. Their sight exceeded that of the seeing! The crowds tried to silence them, but they cried out even louder.

Read Isaiah 29:18 and 35:4–5. What hope did these men have knowing the Messiah was in their midst?

According to prophecy, the messianic age would bring healing to the blind. These men knew the Messiah had come, and He was the fulfillment of their hope. Despite the crowd's annoyance with the blind men, Jesus stopped in the midst of the chaos to ask, "What do you want me to do for you?" He didn't need them to answer. He already knew. The crowd tried to silence them, but Jesus gave them a moment to speak. He elevated these men in front of the people who had dismissed them. Moved with compassion, He touched their eyes and healed them. They looked at the face of the Messiah King they'd been hoping for and followed Him to Jerusalem.

King Jesus still knows your needs. He knows your every thought. And when the world or the enemy tries to silence you from crying out, Jesus still asks, "What do you want me to do for you?" Remember, He's the one who tells you to ask.

What do you want to ask Him for today?

Matthew 21:1–27

◤◥ **READ MATTHEW 21:1-27**

Today's text carries a theme of misunderstanding and unbelief. As you read, look for moments where you see King Jesus being misunderstood and the crowds continuing to doubt the message of His upside-down kingdom.

Jesus, His disciples, and the crowd—likely including the two formerly blind men—continued walking toward Jerusalem. When they arrived at Mount Olives, Jesus sent two of His disciples on an errand to get a donkey and her colt.

Read Zechariah 9:9. How was the King prophesied to appear?

Most kings in ancient times paraded through town on the finest horses, but King Jesus appeared on a young donkey. He entered in meekness—not majesty—on an animal made for service, not battle. In a demonstration of their submission to Him, people threw their cloaks on the ground and waved palm branches, declaring their victory and Jewish nationalism.

Look up the word for *hosanna* (21:9) in a Greek lexicon. What were the crowds asking Jesus to do?

The crowds cried "Hosanna!"— "save us"—as He entered the city of the great King (Psalm 48:1–2). The whole city was stirred up, just like it had been decades before when the King was born (Matthew 2:3). They expected a true king would save them from the oppressive Roman authorities. But their desires were far too small, far too fleeting. King Jesus had His sights set on something far more important than Rome. Yes, He came to save them—but from their sins and from eternal separation from God.

After this misunderstanding, Jesus went to the temple and found people responding improperly to God there as well.

Explain Jesus's words in 21:13. Use a commentary if it's helpful.

Three times per year, people traveled from all over Israel to Jerusalem for holiday celebrations and sacrifices. Having a perfect animal was important according to Jewish law. To accommodate these tourists, the temple complex had a market where the travelers could purchase a spotless animal for their sacrifice. There was also a particular form of currency that was acceptable for the required temple tax. The money-changers acted like many merchants do in tourist hot spots—scamming people with exchange rates and lying about the value of the merchandise.

It seems Jesus didn't have an issue with sales *per se*, but with *robbing* people. The temple was the place that most represented God's generosity to His people, and the merchants were using it as a place to swindle devout tourists.

So much misunderstanding, so much unbelief—yet there were three groups of people who seemed to get it. **Review 21:14–16.** Who were those people?

_____

_____

_____

The Jewish religious leaders were deaf to the message and blind to the mission, but the desperate—the blind and lame—still sought Him, and the children also acknowledged Him rightly, praising Him with messianic speech. As the chief priests and scribes observed this, they grew furious. The tensions of the King were growing, and He left the city for a night of rest in a nearby village.

In the morning, committed to His purpose, He returned to the city. Along the way, He saw a fig tree that had no figs, only leaves. It wasn't the season for figs, after all. Still, Jesus cursed the tree and it withered immediately. He didn't curse the tree because He was entitled or *hangry*; He did it to teach an important message.

Why do you think Jesus cursed the fig tree? **Read Luke 13:6–9 for help. If you have time, see Jeremiah 8:13 and Micah 7:1.**

This fig tree represents the unbelieving among the Jews. Old Testament prophets made this comparison years before. King Jesus desperately wanted Israel to bear fruit, but it hadn't. Of course, there were many Jews who did believe—including His disciples—so this wasn't a rejection of an entire nationality but of those among the Jews who saw His works and didn't yield to His kingship.

Just like the people of the nation didn't believe Him, the leaders of the nation didn't either. **Review 21:23–27.** What two things did they want to know about Jesus?

_____

_____

They were probably still upset about Jesus turning over the tables the day before, and as they questioned Him, King Jesus turned the tables *on them*. He answered their questions with additional questions, but they chose to look ignorant rather than acknowledge that both JTB's and Jesus's authority came from heaven. The chief priests and elders couldn't accept or receive these truths, but they couldn't refute them either.

Tension mounted. As we saw with the fig tree, Jesus has the power to curse as much as to bless. But His humility and submission to the Father's plan kept Him from cursing all who were plotting against Him.

How do Jesus's responses to the crowds spur your heart toward worship?

Matthew 21:28–46

READ MATTHEW 21:28-46

Today we continue the theme of misunderstanding and unbelief. Jesus stood in front of the religious elite and taught in His two favorite ways—asking questions and telling parables. Both parables represent condemnation for the Jews who had rejected Jesus as Messiah.

Review 21:28–32. What general message was Jesus sending in this parable?

One son took his time but was eventually obedient, and the other pretended to be obedient but was disobedient. Jesus made the point that while the prostitutes, tax collectors, and sinners may take a while to be obedient, they're better off than the religious elite who pretend to be obedient but are actually disobedient.

The religious leaders rightly understood the parable, but both the parable and their understanding of it make the same point: Verbal acknowledgment of the truth is not enough—it has to come from a yielded heart. Their hearts refused to accept the truth and enter into the kingdom. And in an affront to everything they believed and valued, Jesus pointed out that even those they deemed lowly—tax collectors and prostitutes—would be welcomed in the kingdom.

Have you ever felt hesitant to obey something you knew God was calling you to do?

What was the result? What did this experience reveal to you about your heart?

He continued with another parable, cranking up the heat as He spoke about wicked tenants, violence, and death. This story opened with a master of a house who carefully established a vineyard before leaving the country and leasing it to tenants. At the right time, the master sent his servants to get his fruit, but the tenants met the servants with brutality. So the master sent additional servants and the violence continued.

Read Jeremiah 20:1–2 and 1 Kings 18:4. Compare the treatment of the servants to the treatment of the Old Testament prophets.

Jesus continued telling the story, announcing the master's plan to send his own son to the vineyard. Surely the tenants wouldn't harm his son! As Jesus shared what was done to the son, the religious leaders were outraged by the wicked tenants' behavior. Jesus set the stage perfectly and invited them into the story by asking them what the master's response should be. It's like Jesus subtly asked them, "What should your punishment be?" And after they told Him what *should* happen, He told them what *would* happen.

Using a dictionary, look up the definition for *cornerstone* and write it below.

What is the significance of Jesus quoting Psalm 118:22–23 in verse 42?

Jesus used this passage to symbolize that He is the rejected stone—the mistreated Son who will receive the prominent position as cornerstone. A cornerstone is the foundational stone of a building; without it, everything falls apart. For many people, the cornerstone of the kingdom was and is a stumbling block—they can't accept Jesus as King. In fact, if we use the comparison of the parable, they throw the son out of his father's vineyard and kill him for their own selfish gain.

In what ways have you "kicked Jesus out" for your own selfish gain?

Instead of repenting, the religious leaders wanted to arrest Jesus but held off for fear of His followers. They continued in unbelief while mistreating and misunderstanding the very Messiah King they'd been waiting for.

Matthew 22

 READ MATTHEW 22

Today's chapter is filled with different groups questioning Jesus, but though they asked questions, they weren't seeking understanding. They were looking for any reason to bring charges against Him. Ultimately, they wanted to put Him to death, but King Jesus knew their motives. He knew the deepest places of their hearts. Unfazed by their wicked intent, He continued proclaiming the message of His upside-down kingdom.

Review Matthew 22:1–14. Summarize the story in your own words.

Which key moments stood out to you?

What point was Jesus trying to drive home for the Pharisees and chief priests?

In this parable, the religious elite could be compared to the invited guests, who refused the king's direct invitation to attend the party honoring the son. The Jews had always been the first ones invited to the party—God first established a covenant with Abraham (Genesis 12:1–3) and declared that the Israelites (Jews) would be His people. But God always knew there would be those among the Jews who resisted His kingship, so the invitation went out to the Gentiles as well. This didn't catch God off guard—it wasn't a shift in His plan, it was *always* His plan (Isaiah 56:3–8, Hosea 2:23). Not only was this idea *not* new in Scripture, but it wasn't new to Jesus's teachings either.

Read Matthew 8:10–12. Who will be cast into outer darkness? Who will be reclining at the table with the patriarchs (Abraham, Isaac, and Jacob)?

Even though the religious leaders certainly knew the Old Testament Scriptures, they hated Jesus for His words. They balked at the idea of the inclusion of outsiders, but His message about their exclusion was more than they could bear. The Pharisees plotted to entrap Him using flattering words and a tricky question.

Review 22:15–17. Use a Bible study resource to learn more about Herodians. What is the significance of the Pharisees and the Herodians approaching Jesus with their question? What is their motive in asking this particular question?

Desperate to catch Jesus doing something wrong, the Pharisees teamed up with another party, the Herodians. These two groups were in total opposition to each other—both politically and religiously—but they joined together to take down their common enemy: King Jesus. The Jews hated giving their money to Rome, but not in the same way that most people dislike paying taxes. Their tax money funded the very army that ruled over them, oppressed them, and even killed their family members. These leaders thought they had found a crafty way to trap Jesus: If He was in favor of paying taxes to Caesar and Rome, He'd lose favor with the tax-burdened people, and if He wasn't, the leaders could accuse Him of rebelling against Rome.

In your own words, summarize the point of Jesus's response to their question about taxes.

How did the religious leaders respond to His answer?

What is your response to authority when you disagree?

Jesus knew His goal wasn't to establish a political kingdom in opposition to Caesar, so He told everyone, "Pay your taxes, obey the civil laws, and submit to the authorities God has placed over you—even if they're wicked and you're in the process of opposing them." Jesus was the perfect example of humbly honoring God while keeping the law and pushing back against wicked authorities. As we strive to imitate Christ, our response should be like His.

Write down the names of leaders in authority over you (your bosses, church leadership, local and national government leaders, etc.). Then take a moment to pray for them all by name.

After the Pharisees and Herodians made their attempt to trap Jesus, the Sadducees—who didn't believe in resurrection—took a swing at discrediting Him. Their plan was to make the idea of resurrection look ridiculous. They cited God's specific instruction for a widow to marry her brother-in-law to protect herself and to provide descendants for the dead man (Deuteronomy 25:5–10), but made the situation more complex.

In your own words, summarize the point of Jesus's response to their question.

How did the crowd respond to Jesus's answer?

Jesus quoted Exodus 3:6 and drove home the reality that the covenants made with Abraham, Isaac, and Jacob didn't stop once the men died. God has the power to resurrect the patriarchs (and all His people) to enjoy Him eternally. This was a mic-drop moment. Jesus left them dumbfounded.

After hearing that Jesus had silenced the Sadducees, the Pharisees wanted to try again. A Pharisee who was also a lawyer asked Jesus which commandment was the most important. Jesus encapsulated all 613 Old Testament laws into just two—the vertical or "man to God" laws, and the horizontal or "man to man" laws. Jesus didn't *eliminate* any of God's commands—He just summarized them. Mark 12's account tells us that the man was impressed and that Jesus told him, "You are not far from the kingdom of God" (Mark 12:34). This was true in both a spiritual and a literal sense—because the very King of the kingdom was speaking to him.

Which of these two commandments is easier for you to follow?

☐ You shall love the Lord your God with all your heart and with all your soul and with all your mind.

☐ You shall love your neighbor as yourself.

If you were to stop obeying the one that is more difficult for you, how would that impact you and the world around you?

Summarize 22:41–46 in your own words. Which person(s) of the Trinity does the passage reference?

Jesus continued His Q&A session by responding to some who were perplexed that the Messiah could be both a descendant of David and somehow pre-date David as well. These verses give us a lens on what it means for Jesus, God the Son, to be outside of time—to have existed *always*. He existed before David, who died a thousand years earlier, even though Jesus was only about thirty-three years old at the time of this conversation. Jesus also affirmed that this psalm was written by David via the Holy Spirit. Don't miss this important moment: *God the Son confirmed that God the Spirit authored Scripture through human hands!*

Despite the ill motives of the crowd and the difficulty of the questions, King Jesus had the authority and ability to answer. He remained humble while displaying great knowledge, and He remained steadfast in proclaiming the message of His upside-down kingdom. He invites us into this posture too, and following His lead is where we'll thrive and find peace! He's where the joy is!

What stood out to you most in this week's study? Why?

What did you learn or relearn about God and His character this week?

DAY 6

Corresponding Psalm & Prayer

 READ PSALM 118

What correlation do you see between Psalm 118 and this week's study of Jesus and His kingdom?

What portions stand out to you most?

Close by praying this prayer aloud:

> *Father,*
>   *As the psalmist said, "You are my God, and I will give thanks to you; you are my God; I will extol you." I praise You for Your righteousness and for opening the gates of the kingdom to me. Your*

generosity to sinners reveals the tenderness of Your heart, and I praise You for it!

I am a sinner, and I appeal to Your mercy. At times, I have leaned into my unbelief and rebelled. I have not sought You or Your ways. I've been tempted to ask questions without having a heart to truly understand. I've resisted Your commands to love You and others, and I've focused on loving myself. Father, I repent of my sins and turn to You and ask You to make my heart clean.

Help me, Spirit. Grant me a heart that loves You first and foremost. Grant me a heart that loves my neighbors and even those who could be considered my enemies. Grant me faith in the spaces where I don't understand Your will or Your ways. Equip me with obedience to follow You.

I surrender my life to You, Lord—every moment of my day, each decision I make, I yield my will and way to Your perfect will and way.

I love You too. Amen.

Rest, Catch Up, or Dig Deeper

 WEEKLY CHALLENGE

On Day 1, we read 1 Corinthians 10:6–10 and Philippians 2:14 and noted the warnings about grumbling. Grumbling is *so* detrimental to us—not just as Christ-followers but as humans. In fact, researchers have found that frequent complaining can damage the hippocampus, the region of the brain responsible for cognitive functioning.*

Scripture repeatedly reminds us that God's commands are for our good. His command not to grumble or complain is for our good! In ways He has always known but science only recently discovered, following His commands promotes our health and thriving. Obeying God actually promotes brain health!

This week, be mindful of your words. Aim to eliminate grumbling and complaining. Ask those you spend the most time with to point it out to you when you slip up, then be quick to repent. Aim to fill your words with praise and gratitude. Keep a gratitude list if it's helpful for you—either in your journal or through a piece of art you create throughout the week. Be as creative and colorful as you want!

*Stephanie Vozza, "Why Complaining May Be Dangerous to Your Health," Fast Company, January 12, 2015, https://www.fastcompany.com/3040672/why-complaining-may-be-dangerous -to-your-health.

Matthew 23–25:
Discourse of the King

DAILY BIBLE READING

Day 1: Matthew 23

Day 2: Matthew 24:1–28

Day 3: Matthew 24:29–51

Day 4: Matthew 25:1–30

Day 5: Matthew 25:31–46

Day 6: Psalm 50

Day 7: Catch-Up Day

Corresponds to Days 309 and 311–312 of *The Bible Recap*.

WEEKLY CHALLENGE

See page 202 for more information.

Matthew 23

 READ MATTHEW 23

Pick three to five words that best describe the attitudes and actions of the scribes and Pharisees based on what you've seen in Scripture.

Your chosen words may paint a not-so-positive picture of Israel's religious leaders. In today's reading, Jesus adds the finishing touches to a tragic portrait of the Pharisees and scribes.

Using a Bible dictionary, look up the terms *scribe* and *Pharisee*. What were the role and significance of each in Jewish society?

In your own words, briefly summarize why Jesus and these religious leaders experienced ongoing tension.

Jesus publicly pronounced woe—a prophetic indictment of behavior that leads to tragedy—on the scribes and Pharisees. But before He dug in, Jesus started with something that might have surprised you—and them—given what He'd said about these leaders so far. He called the people to listen to and obey what the Pharisees taught because the Pharisees sat on Moses's seat.

Why does Jesus bring up Moses's seat? What is its relevance, and why should it have motivated the people to obey the scribes and Pharisees?

It wasn't a one-to-one comparison, but the scribes and Pharisees held a position of interpreting and enforcing the law, which resembled Moses's role since he was the one who first brought God's law to the people. Jesus distinguished between authority given by God and actions that dishonor God carried out by those in authority. God's law was still good and perfect even though the Pharisees' lives presented a distorted view of it. Jesus exposed the unrighteousness of these religious leaders who crushed the people under heavy spiritual burdens and operated out of their desire to be seen and praised by people. He called His disciples to live differently.

Compare Matthew 23:4–12 and Philippians 2:1–11. Make note of your observations below.

Examples to Avoid:

Matthew 23:4 _____

Matthew 23:5–7 _____

How Jesus Calls His Followers to Live:

Matthew 23:8–10 _____

Matthew 23:11 _____

Matthew 23:12 _____

Example to Imitate:

Philippians 2:4–7 _____

Philippians 2:8 _____

Jesus was the perfect example of everything He preached. He was speaking to the crowds and against the Pharisees from a place of authority as King and from His lived experience as a sacrificial servant.

Jesus spoke seven woes to the scribes and Pharisees, offering a specific list of how they had gone astray and impacted others in the process.

Read the woes that Jesus pronounced on the scribes and Pharisees and summarize the actions and attitudes Jesus condemned them for.

1. _____

2. _____

3. _____

4. _____

5. _____

6. _____

7. _____

What common themes do you notice?

Jesus told the scribes and Pharisees that sorrow awaited them because they were acting as functional barriers, keeping people out of the kingdom while not even entering it themselves. They focused on tiny technicalities and emphasized nonessentials while minimizing what truly mattered to the heart of God. Despite their attempts to appear externally clean, Jesus said they were internally corrupt. He denounced them for celebrating the prophets and righteous men their ancestors killed as if they weren't following in their ancestors' footsteps. And in pointing this out, He alluded to the role they would play in His impending death.

In the ESV, the section header over 23:37–39 is "Lament over Jerusalem." In your own words, describe what it means to lament. **Read Psalm 35:13–14, Jeremiah 14:1–3, and Matthew 2:16–18 to help with your answer.**

Jesus's last woe led into His lament. As He thought about the spiritual state of Jerusalem, He experienced soul-wrenching grief. While He wanted to draw them into His kingdom, they wanted Him dead. Given all Jesus's harsh words toward the religious leaders, we might expect Him to have a cold, callous attitude toward them, but instead we see a King whose heart is still tender toward those unwilling to turn to Him.

How do you respond to those in your life who oppose God? Are you cynical? Indifferent? Do you grieve?

If your heart posture is out of alignment with the King and His kingdom values, write out a prayer below asking Him to give you His heart for those outside the kingdom.

Matthew 24:1–28

◤ READ MATTHEW 24:1-28

With thoughts of Jerusalem likely still in mind, Jesus and His disciples left the temple and headed toward Mount Olives, just outside the city gates, where He offered some intense details about what was to come. While the disciples admired the beauty of the buildings, Jesus broke the news that the temple would come tumbling down in the not-too-distant future. The temple was a huge complex built with massive stones—the largest of which weighed more than one million pounds. This was no damage-prone, rinky-dink structure, yet fewer than forty years later, the Roman army toppled the temple and fulfilled His words.

Whether they were shocked, confused, or unbelieving, the disciples would've had a reaction to this information. The temple was a central element of Jewish religious life and culture. But Jesus seemed to deliver the news like it was no big deal.

Read Revelation 21:22. What did Jesus know about the future of Israel's worship that allowed Him to be so calm about the temple's destruction?

As a physical building, the temple was always meant to be temporary. God had instituted it with an expiration date. It was never intended to be His permanent home, so its destruction was a necessary part of fully ushering in His unshakeable, eternal kingdom.

When they got to their destination, the disciples started peppering Jesus with questions: *When was this destruction going to happen? He alluded to going away, but when was He coming back? Was He going to tell them when the end of the world would be?*

Review Jesus's response to the disciples in 24:3–28. Look for every usage of the words *will* and *when*.

What did Jesus say would certainly happen?

Did He repeat or emphasize anything? If so, what?

Did Jesus offer a specific time when something would take place?

Instead of telling them to mark their calendars, Jesus explained what they should expect to see happening. Terrible events would begin to ramp up, and they would think it was the end, but that would only be the beginning of the trying times.

He reminded them about the abomination of desolation, which Daniel had prophesied about (Daniel 9:27, 11:31, 12:11). The Greek word for *abomination* (*bdelygma*) means something detestable or foul, and it was typically used in the context of idolatry. Jesus was pointing toward a grievous and offensive act of idolatry that would happen in God's holy place. That event would lead to devastation and destruction.

In the account, Matthew inserted the aside "let the reader understand." And to this day, readers are still trying to understand this prophecy. Some scholars think this event has already happened (after Jesus spoke these words but prior to today), while others believe its fulfillment is still yet to come. In either scenario, the information and instruction Jesus left for His followers remain the same.

Review 24:3–28. Write down every directive aimed at the disciples. If Jesus gives a "why," make note of that too.

Jesus said the end of the age would be the most difficult time the world ever had seen or ever would see. He didn't shy away from the gravity of the situation. But He also didn't seem to be stuck on the horrific events that would unfold. Much like us, the disciples likely wanted more details than Jesus disclosed. Perhaps they began to spiral into worry over hypotheticals. But Jesus didn't want them to be concerned in that way.

There are two primary ways a person can be concerned. Being "concerned *about*" is to lean into worry or fear, whereas being "concerned *with*" is to be involved and invested and to give attention to something.

With those definitions and Jesus's teaching and priorities in mind, what was Jesus telling His disciples to be *concerned with*?

What did He direct them away from being *concerned about*?

What might this mean for a follower of Jesus today? What parallels can you draw to things God might desire for you to be more concerned *with* and less concerned *about* in your own life?

Although Jesus was speaking about the dark days ahead, He wove clear glimpses of light into His words. Despite the difficulties that would result in many being led astray or falling away, there would be people who would endure in faith. The good news of salvation wasn't going to stay local or even regional; in fact, it would go out to the whole world just as God's prophets foretold throughout the Old Testament. And He gave assurance that the hard times would pass and He would return for His elect—those who would persevere by His power until the end!

Matthew 24:29–51

READ MATTHEW 24:29-51

Review 24:29. Do you believe this verse points to a literal or symbolic event? What do you think it means?

The cosmic signs that Jesus mentioned in today's reading could be figurative, literal, or both. But in any case, He was emphasizing that there would be major disturbances to everyday life and order that would be impossible to ignore, and they would usher in His glorious arrival. The Son of Man would make His awaited return, riding on the clouds, accompanied by angels, and set to a trumpet blast soundtrack. His angels would be sent out to the ends of the earth to gather His people—those whose lives were marked by genuine faith.

The following verses are all connected to Jesus's words in 24:30–31. **Read each passage,** note the connection, and write down anything it emphasizes or adds to your understanding.

Zechariah 12:10–14	
Daniel 7:13–14	
Revelation 1:7	

While Jesus didn't disclose the specific details of exactly when He would come back—information that even He wasn't privy to—He gave the disciples a good idea of what it would be like and what it would look like for His followers to wait well.

Jesus said that just as a fig tree's budding branches were nature's sign that summer was on its way, all the events He described would be how His followers could discern that the Son of Man was on His way. More than just something to anticipate or be aware of, Jesus made it clear that His second coming was something to prepare for.

What do you think preparing for His return entails?

To continue painting the picture, Jesus pointed back to the days of Noah and the worldwide flood, which came unexpectedly for most. Like the sudden nature of that life-changing event, people would be going about business as usual, eating meals, celebrating marriages, and working jobs when He returned. Some people would be gathered to Him, and others would face the harsh opposing reality. In light of it all, Jesus's charge was to expect the unexpected—to stay awake and always be ready.

Read 1 Thessalonians 5:1–11. What similarities do you see between this passage and what Jesus said to His disciples in Matthew 24 about His return and the end of the age?

In 1 Thessalonians 5:1–11, what does the writer (Paul) say about who His readers are and are not?

What are they called to do and not do in light of those realities?

It's clear that Jesus didn't want the disciples to miss the heart of what it means to wait well, because instead of moving on from the topic they'd already spent a reasonable amount of time discussing, He dove in deeper through a short parable. He showed them the stark contrast between the lives of a faithful servant and a wicked one—including their actions and the resulting ends.

Though we live in a different time and culture, Jesus's call to stay awake and ready (24:42–44) applies to everyone living before His return. How can you live as a faithful and wise servant waiting for your Master?

Jesus never wasted time or words; in every moment He spent with the crowds or His disciples, He meaningfully illuminated spiritual truths—He demonstrated righteousness, revealed His authority, warned about coming judgment, called to repentance, and pointed people to the kingdom to come. And while the disciples might not have known it then, Jesus knew that the countdown clock to His crucifixion was quickly approaching zero—making every sentence spoken and every second spent with them especially significant.

Jesus was focused on communicating truth that would lead toward eternal life. His utmost priority was preparing people to inherit His kingdom, and nothing could sidetrack Him. Jesus *will* return in power and glory, and for all those who trust in Him—past, present, and future—it will have been worth whatever they endured in the wait!

Matthew 25:1–30

◣ READ MATTHEW 25:1–30

In today's reading, Jesus presented His disciples with the same food for thought, served on two different plates. His focus remained on the coming of the kingdom as He turned back to parables as His teaching tool of choice. Today's parables share the theme of being ready for His return. Since this was the last week of His life before His crucifixion, Jesus wanted to drive this message home.

His first lesson introduced us to ten virgins with lamps. The virgins of ancient times were similar to the bridesmaids of today. Traditional Jewish weddings had three parts: engagement, betrothal, and marriage ceremony. The couple had to endure a long period of waiting between the betrothal and the marriage ceremony.

In this parable, the bridesmaids were supposed to go meet the groom, but when he took longer than expected, they fell asleep. They were startled awake by shouts at midnight announcing his arrival. Out of the ten, half were called foolish and half were called wise, based on whether they were prepared.

What did all ten bridesmaids have in common?

In your own words, describe how the parable played out for the foolish bridesmaids.

When it was time for the marriage feast, only the five wise women were present. They were ready when the groom arrived, and they entered the marriage feast with him as members of his wedding party. They were the only ones the groom recognized. The foolish, unprepared bridesmaids were left outside the celebration.

Jesus was emphasizing that those who will be with Him in His kingdom are not just those who expect His eventual arrival but those who are ready for Him regardless of when He comes.

The parable of the talents sends a similar message. In ancient Israel, a talent was a type of currency, not an ability. So for clarity's sake, we'll call this the parable of the dollars. Jesus told about a master who was leaving on an extended trip and entrusting His money to three of His servants based on their individual abilities. The master expected a return on investment from each servant.

Fill in the table below.

	Servant with $1	Servant with $2	Servant with $5
What does he do while the master is gone?			
How does the master respond to him upon his return?			
What does he receive from the master?			

Review 25:24. How did the servant with one dollar describe the master?

Review 25:25. How did the servant with one dollar feel as a result of his view of the master?

What did the master invite the servants given two and five dollars to be part of?

The master severely punished the servant who mistrusted his heart, and cast him out. The master never affirmed that his character was what the servant feared—he posed a question to the servant about it. His true character was revealed in how he responded to the other two servants, who trusted his heart. He generously rewarded them and invited them to share in his abundance and joy!

Describe a time when you feared the Master instead of leaning into the joy of faithful service.

In these parables, Jesus made it clear that judgment will be a part of His return. We should be ready to be evaluated.

Read Romans 3:23–24, Romans 3:28, 1 Corinthians 1:30–31, Galatians 2:15–16, and Ephesians 2:8–9. What standard will we be evaluated by when Christ returns?

Describe how that makes you feel. Why?

Those who are in Christ don't need to fear His judgment because, while perfect righteousness is the standard we will be evaluated by, He has accomplished perfect righteousness on our behalf. He has granted us His righteousness and taken our sin and shame. Praise Christ—we never need to fear falling short of His standard if we are relying on His works instead of our own!

Matthew 25:31–46

READ MATTHEW 25:31–46

The return of Jesus will be a great and glorious event marked by rejoicing for some and regret for others. The Son of Man will be seated on His throne, surrounded by the angels, who will be singing His praises for all eternity. He's poised to pronounce judgment on all nations gathered before His throne.

But before He speaks a single word of reward or punishment, He will begin the work of separating—dividing those who will inherit His everlasting kingdom from those who will experience eternal punishment. The King will put the sheep (believers) on His right and the goats (unbelievers) on His left. This wasn't the first time Jesus described Himself using shepherd imagery.

Read Matthew 9:36 and Psalm 23. What aspects of Jesus as Shepherd King stand out to you as they apply to the final judgment?

The King addressed the sheep first. In just a few words, He spoke volumes about the beauty of the reward they'll receive and the nature of salvation. Scripture uses several terms to refer to these sheep—including children, heirs, and faithful servants.

Write 25:34 below. Circle the one who is doing the blessing.

When was this blessing prepared?

Look up Ephesians 1:3. Who is doing the blessing? Who is blessed? Through whom does the blessing come?

Look up Romans 8:16–17. Who bears witness to the inheritance of God's children?

Scripture points to a plan and a purpose from before time began. In the eternal plan of salvation, the three persons of the Trinity work together as a team, but each person plays distinct roles in carrying out our salvation and granting us our inheritance.

What does the King list as evidence that the righteous sheep are righteous?

What does the King list as evidence the unrighteous goats are unrighteous?

Jesus said that our actions toward others, especially those who are in positions of weakness, reflect our hearts toward Him.

What does this reveal about the King?

Both the righteous and the unrighteous were surprised when the King pointed out their actions, almost as if they were living on autopilot, doing what was naturally in their hearts. Our hearts are revealed in our actions, and God sees our motives, thoughts, and intentions, even before they become actions (Psalm 139:1–4). He rewards those who are motivated not by being seen, but by their hidden heart (Matthew 6:1–4).

Read Hosea 6:6, Psalm 51:16–17, and Amos 5:21–24. List out the things God was looking for from His people.

Even in the Old Testament, we see the same thread. What Jesus revealed about the kingdom has always been true. The rules haven't changed. The King has always been after the hearts of His people. And in the final judgment, the King will reveal the hearts of all mankind. As we wrap up this week, we would be wise to examine our own hearts to see if we are in the faith.

Read the following verses and write down anything that stands out to you.

- 2 Corinthians 13:5 _____

- John 20:31 _____

- 1 John 5:12 _____

- Romans 8:16–17 _____

Scripture says we should test ourselves to see if we are in the faith (2 Corinthians 13:5). A test implies an answer. If you're uncertain of the answer, search your heart and the Scriptures and ask God to bring clarity. This is an invitation into greater truth, freedom, and joy—as well as into the eternal kingdom. The King longs for you to be there with Him, where His presence is the greatest inheritance of all, because He's where the joy is!

What stood out to you most in this week's study? Why?

What did you learn or relearn about God and His character this week?

DAY 6

Corresponding
Psalm & Prayer

 **READ PSALM 50**

What correlation do you see between Psalm 50 and this week's study of Jesus and His kingdom?

What portions stand out to you most?

Close by praying this prayer aloud:

Father,
    I praise You for Your righteousness. You are perfect and just in all Your ways. While it can be terrifying to realize I'll never live up to Your standard, I'm eternally grateful that You provided a way for

that righteousness to be granted to me, through no effort of my own. Jesus, thank You for living a perfect life and trading it for my sin. Because Your righteousness was assigned to me, I can approach the Father with confidence, knowing I'm His child and I'm welcomed with celebration in His eternal kingdom of joy!

Father, I have sinned, and I appeal to Your mercy. I confess that I've viewed You wrongly at times. Like the servant with one dollar, I've mistrusted Your heart, leading me to spiral into self-protection. I've tried to earn my own righteousness. Like the scribes and Pharisees, I've wanted to be noticed and respected for my actions. I've wanted to impress You and others. I've put the focus on whatever things I can manage to do well, but there are so many areas where I still fail. And underneath even my good actions, my heart is still bent inward. I've been selfishly ambitious instead of surrendering to the righteousness of Christ. I repent of my sins and turn to You and ask You to make my heart clean.

Help me to find rest—true rest—in knowing that Jesus has accomplished all You require of me. Help me to view You rightly. Grant me wisdom to know how to prepare well, like the wise virgins and servants. Where I fear the return of Your Son, Jesus, or have disregarded His words or have just lived my life recklessly as if He's never coming back, fix my heart. Grant me an eager desire for His return!

I surrender my life to You, Lord—every moment of my day, each decision I make, I yield my will and way to Your perfect will and way.

I love You too. Amen.

Rest, Catch Up, or Dig Deeper

WEEKLY CHALLENGE

In Matthew 23:5–7, Jesus spoke out against the scribes and Pharisees for being motivated by pride and praise, and He warned against following in their footsteps. Even though we don't live among Pharisees today, this is still a relevant issue. As Christians, we can easily slip into the same kinds of attitudes and actions if we're not careful. We can do spiritual things for attention, applause, or status, rather than simply serving God and loving others out of a heart of gratitude and joy.

How can we tackle this temptation to live like Pharisees? Jesus presented a solution in Matthew 23:8–11. When we let go of glory-seeking, give God His rightful praise, and take hold of humility, we're walking in the way Jesus laid out.

This week our challenge is to put the wisdom of Matthew 23:8–11 into practice daily. As you walk through this week, ask God to make you aware of any area where you're acting out of a desire for acknowledgment or admiration.

Whenever you sense that your heart is bent inward toward yourself, confess it to God. Then pray the words of Psalm 115:1: "Not to us, O LORD, not to us, but to your name give glory, for the sake of your steadfast love and your faithfulness!" Write the words on a note in your phone or on a three-by-five card that you can keep in a place where you'll see it regularly. This will serve as a reminder that He is a better and more fitting motivator than selfish gain!

The act of shining a light on wrong motivations and shifting your attention to the Lord with reverence, repentance, and worship will help rewire your heart and mind!

┌─ Scripture to Memorize ─┐

But seek first the king-
dom of God and his righ-
teousness, and all these
things will be added to you.

Matthew 6:33
└─────────────────────┘

Matthew 26:
Betrayal of the King

DAILY BIBLE READING

Day 1: Matthew 26:1–16

Day 2: Matthew 26:17–29

Day 3: Matthew 26:30–46

Day 4: Matthew 26:47–68

Day 5: Matthew 26:69–75

Day 6: Psalm 55

Day 7: Catch-Up Day

Corresponds to Day 313 of *The Bible Recap*.

WEEKLY CHALLENGE

See page 225 for more information.

Matthew 26:1–16

 READ MATTHEW 26:1–16

Review 26:1–2. What are some of the specific details Jesus revealed about His death?

Read John 18:4. How much did Jesus know about His death in advance?

Read Revelation 13:8. How long has Jesus's death been planned? Given that timeline, who made the original plan for Jesus's death?

In today's reading, Jesus dropped a bombshell on His disciples, telling them the exact timeline and manner of His death. The authorities were already plotting it, in fact, which had them falling in line with God's plan from before the foundation of the earth.

Read Daniel 2:21, Romans 13:1, and John 19:11. Who should be credited with establishing the rulers who were responsible for Jesus's death?

The chief priests and the elders may have been the rulers du jour, but God is the one on the highest throne eternally. The people in charge of earthly kingdoms still fall under the authority of His eternal kingdom, where He sovereignly reigns and is working out His loving plan to redeem His people and restore the broken relationship with them. These rulers, without even knowing it, were participating in God's plan for His glory, Christ's praise, and our freedom and joy!

While Jesus was in Jerusalem for the holiday, He went to a dinner party hosted by Simon the leper in Bethany, a village just outside the city walls.

Look up the verses below and list the known dinner party attendees.

Matthew 26:6 _____

Matthew 26:8 _____

John 12:2 _____

John 12:3 _____

John 12:4 _____

What does it reveal about Jesus that He would spend some of His final hours before His death dining in this company—a leper, women, and the man He knew would betray Him?

Think about the company you keep. Are there people in your circle who are different from you or who might be "risky" to spend time with? How can you discern whether it is wise or foolish to spend time with a person like that?

From John's account, we learn that Mary is the person who anointed Jesus (John 12:3), using an oil made of pure nard. This kind of oil was most often used for acts of devotion and was incredibly pricy. Judas objected to Mary's use of the oil (John 12:4–7), but Jesus replied with compassion toward her. He said this story would be told all over the world—and here we are, two thousand years later, still talking about it. How beautiful that in the midst of this story about His final days, Jesus took the time to highlight the offering of a woman—someone who had little value in that culture. It has always been like Jesus to see the lesser, the outcast, and to remind them of their value to God (10:31). Then He plainly indicated, yet again, that He was about to die. He said Mary was preparing Him for His burial.

Judas knew the rulers wanted to arrest Jesus, so he seized the opportunity to make thirty pieces of silver by turning Jesus in. The Passover was approaching, and the rulers agreed not to arrest Jesus during the feast, because it would've stirred up too much trouble.

Read John 12:1–7. Based on what John says about Judas's character, how might Mary's use of the expensive oil have played a role in Judas's decision to betray Jesus?

In the final hours before His death, Jesus encountered both extravagant worship and deep betrayal. Despite the range of emotions He must've experienced, He kept both of these groups of people close to Him as He moved, undeterred, toward fulfilling the Father's eternal plan.

Matthew 26:17–29

▲ **READ MATTHEW 26:17-29**

Jesus instructed His disciples on how to plan for the meal they were about to eat. At dinner, He announced that there was a betrayer among them. They were mortified, each wondering if it could be him. They all knew that they had the capacity to betray Jesus.

Read 26:22–25. How is Judas's question different from the question the other apostles asked? What significance does this hold?

All the other disciples asked, "Is it I, Lord?" but Judas asked a different question. He asked, "Is it I, Rabbi?" He called Jesus "teacher," not "master." Jesus affirmed that yes, Judas was the one who would betray Him. But Judas wasn't shocked by this news; he already had the silver in his possession.

As with most things, there are passive and active agents involved in bringing God's will to pass. Judas was the active agent in this particular story.

What role did you play in Christ's death? Why is it important to acknowledge our role?

We are all passive agents in Christ's death. As for Judas, verse 24 says it would've been better for him if he hadn't been born, but his birth was a necessary part of God's redemption plan. While we may be tempted to feel sorry for Judas, it's important to remember that he got exactly what he deserved—what we *all* deserve, in fact. Jesus, on the other hand, did *not* get what He deserved. He took the penalty we earned through our sin and rebellion.

After His brief conversation with Judas, Jesus served what we call the Lord's Supper or Communion or the Eucharist—which means "to give thanks"—and in doing this, He gave them a physical action that connected them to a spiritual reality, much like with baptism. This sacrament helps to remind us how His body was broken and His blood was poured out for many people. Jesus invited all the disciples to participate, even Judas. Perhaps one reason Judas was included was to demonstrate that participation in Communion isn't salvific.

How often do you and your church or family participate in this sacrament? Describe what the process is like for you spiritually and emotionally.

Read 26:26–29. What items are mentioned as a part of the Passover meal Jesus and His disciples ate?

Exodus 12:1–28 tells the story of God establishing the Passover. Read the whole passage if you have time. **Look at Exodus 12:15.** What item is supposed to be avoided during this feast? What is the punishment for eating this item?

Using a Greek lexicon, look up the word for *bread* **in Matthew 26:17** and write down what you find.

Using a Greek lexicon, look up the word for *bread* **in Matthew 26:26** and write down what you find.

It is highly significant that the only items mentioned at the Last Supper are bread and wine. The Passover Feast consisted of several elements, the most crucial of which was the Passover lamb. Eating it was a command, so why was it absent? It's also significant that Scripture says Jesus and His disciples were eating *leavened* bread (Greek: *artos*), which was forbidden during the Feast of Unleavened Bread (Greek: *azymos*). Where was the *unleavened* bread the law requires?

Here's one theory on why those two crucial aspects of a Passover Feast seem to be missing. The Feast of Unleavened Bread was typically a week-long celebration, but some scholars say that in Jesus's day it was actually an eight-day celebration, with the additional day being tacked on before the start of the week. During the seven days of the actual event, the Jews weren't allowed to eat anything with leaven in it, so adding a "day zero" at the start gave them a chance to finish off all the existing leaven in their homes before the formal seven-day event actually began.

If that's true, then when Jesus and His disciples were having what we've typically thought of as *the* Passover Feast, it may have just been *a* Passover Feast—where they're kind of "cleaning out the fridge." It's their final leavened feast before the unleavened feast begins. And that would explain why they didn't eat lamb either. And it would be fitting, because when Jesus was slaughtered on the following day before the feast began, He became *the* Passover Lamb (1 Corinthians 5:7, Revelation 5:9). We'll study this event more next week, but for now, praise Jesus for covering our sins!

Matthew 26:30–46

◤ **READ MATTHEW 26:30–46**

After they ate the bread and drank the wine of the Last Supper, Jesus and His disciples sang a hymn, then headed to Mount Olives, which is a hill just a short walk outside the Eastern Gate of Jerusalem's city walls. Jesus had just foretold Judas's betrayal, but suddenly He had another round of bad news for His followers: They would *all* fall away that night because of Him.

Review 26:31. Look up the phrase *fall away* in a Greek lexicon and write down what you find.

At dinner, only an hour or so earlier, they had all asked if they would be the ones to betray Him, but somehow they seemed shocked to hear Him say they would deny Him. Jesus also told Peter that he'd deny Him three times. Peter was dismayed and said he'd never deny Jesus; in fact, he'd even be willing to die with Him! The other disciples who were there echoed his words. (We can infer that Judas was not among the disciples at that point, because he showed up later with the soldiers who came to arrest Jesus.)

At the bottom of Mount Olives, there was a garden filled with olive trees where the olives were pressed for oil. It's still there today, in fact.

Review 26:36. Look up the word *Gethsemane* in a Greek lexicon and write down what you find.

This was the place where olives were crushed to extract what is most valuable from them. So it's fitting that it was also the place where Jesus experienced the crushing weight of His pending death—in which He would offer mankind the most valuable gift we could ever receive.

As Jesus prayed in the garden, He invited some of His closest friends into His grief. He asked James, John, and even Peter—the one He had just identified as His soon-to-be denier—to stay with Him in the garden as He prayed. He went off a little farther and asked the Father if there was any other way this plan could be accomplished. He knew the answer was no.

Read Hebrews 9:22 and 10:1–10. Why is the old sacrificial system (the one God established in the Old Testament) insufficient?

Animal sacrifices were offered repeatedly, and they were always intended to be temporary (Hebrews 10:1–4). God had always been pointing toward the *perfect, final* sacrifice. While an imperfect man could die for his own sins, offering a one-to-one exchange, only a perfect man could die for the sins of many. The only way sinful mankind could be reconciled to a holy God was through the death of a perfect man, and there has only ever been one perfect Man—Jesus, our Messiah King.

Jesus knew that His death would be unbelievably painful and gruesome. He dreaded it, but after asking the Father three times if there might be another way, Jesus surrendered to the Father's plan. Though Jesus is fully God, He is also fully man. His earthly nature had to submit to His divine nature. He prayed, "Not my will but Yours be done." That's a good way to pray when you know God's answer is no, because God still invites us to share our hearts with Him. No desire and no darkness surprise Him—after all, He already knows our hearts (Psalm 139:23–24). Jesus demonstrated what it's like to hold the tension of pouring your heart out to God while still surrendering.

Have you ever asked God for something that you knew was not part of His plan for you? What was the process of surrender like for you?

As Jesus stayed in the garden grieving, praying, and surrendering, He looked up toward the city walls and saw Judas and the team of soldiers coming to arrest Him. Since it was dark, they carried torches (see John 18:3) as they made their way through the valley and into the garden. Hypothetically, if Jesus wanted to, He could've run the other direction, up to the top of Mount Olives, and fled into the Judean wilderness, which starts just on the other side of the hill. But He didn't. He stayed. He willingly surrendered as He was betrayed into the hands of sinners.

Jesus knows what it's like to be you. He knows what it's like to dread the future, to be betrayed by your friends, to grieve losses. He not only paid the penalty for our sins, but He took on flesh to know our ache in a very real way. What a gift to have a King like Him, who enters into the pain of His people.

Matthew 26:47–68

◣ READ MATTHEW 26:47-68

As Jesus was telling His disciples that His betrayer was at hand, Judas approached with an armed crowd. Judas had told them he would indicate which one was Jesus by kissing Him—a common greeting in that day. Again, Judas called Jesus *Rabbi* (Teacher) instead of *Master* (Lord), just as he had at the Last Supper. And Jesus replied by calling Judas *friend*— but not using the typical word for *friend* (*philos*); instead, Jesus used the variation that implies more of an acquaintance (*hetairos*). It's only used two other times in Scripture—both times in parables where Jesus referenced wicked people who were taking advantage of a righteous person. And that's exactly what Judas was doing.

Jesus knew what was about to happen, and He submitted to it. As the soldiers began to take Him away, Peter pulled out his sword to launch a counterattack, cutting off the ear of a man named Malchus, who was a servant to the high priest (John 18:10).

Read Matthew 10:34. It's possible that Peter was recalling these words of Jesus. Based on our study of Matthew 10, explain why Peter's response wasn't aligned with Jesus's teaching.

Jesus put a stop to Peter's actions and reminded him that He could have asked the Father to send a massive number of angels (roughly 60,000–72,000) to war on His behalf if He were interested in fighting back. Instead, He submitted.

Review 26:54 and 26:56. What is Jesus focused on?

Jesus knew the cross was the only way, and He was intent on Scripture being fulfilled. He wasn't interested in putting up a fight. In Luke's account of this story, Jesus even healed Malchus's ear after Peter cut it off (Luke 22:51).

Read Matthew 5:11–12. In Jesus's first sermon, He taught His followers how to respond in circumstances like this. What did He tell them to do?

How do you tend to respond when people wrongly accuse you or misunderstand you? If responding righteously is a challenge for you, what can you take from these verses or the example of Jesus that might help you grow in this area?

After He was seized, the disciples fell away, just as He'd promised. The soldiers led Jesus to His trial before Caiaphas, the high priest, who was joined by all the religious leaders. Peter followed, keeping his distance, and sat through the trial alongside the enemies of Jesus. The leaders sought people to give false testimony, but at first no one gave a testimony that incriminated Jesus.

Review 26:60–61. What did these witnesses accuse Jesus of saying? Why would this have been a problem for Caiaphas and the religious leaders?

Read John 2:18–21. How is what Jesus actually said different from what He was accused of saying (in Matthew 26:60–61)?

What Jesus Said	The Accusation

What was Jesus referring to when He made the statement the witnesses were recalling?

Read Isaiah 53:7. How was Jesus's response to Caiaphas in 26:62–63 consistent with this prophecy?

Read Matthew 16:13–17. Who is the Son of Man?

Jesus was accused of threatening to destroy the temple, but He had actually said someone else would destroy it, and He would be the one to raise it back up in three days. He was referring not to the temple where they worshiped, but the temple of His body. The temple is the place where God came to dwell with mankind, so it's fitting that Jesus—God incarnate—would refer to His own body as the temple.

He also referenced (what appears to be) His favorite name for Himself: the Son of Man. He told them He would be seated with the Father in the heavenlies. To the high priest, who didn't regard Jesus as God, this sounded like blasphemy. The leaders agreed, handing down a guilty verdict—and they believed He deserved the death penalty as His punishment. He was beaten, slapped, and spat on as they taunted Him.

He endured many rounds of questioning, accusations, and abuse, and through it all He still walked in His authority as King. He spoke the truth when necessary, He was silent when necessary, and He continued to walk out the Father's plan, taking one more step toward the cross with each conversation. This had been His mission all along, and it was approaching its fulfillment.

Matthew 26:69–75

◥◤ **READ MATTHEW 26:69-75**

Even today, if you walk through the old city of Jerusalem, you'll hear roosters crowing. It's a frequent reminder of the things our King endured in the final hours before His death. It can transport you back to the night of His arrest, when one of His closest companions fulfilled His prophecy by denying Him three times.

After Peter watched Jesus's trial in front of Caiaphas, he sat outside in the courtyard where the trial had taken place. Others were gathered there, and when one girl recognized Peter as a follower of Jesus, he denied it. Possibly fearing he had been exposed, he moved toward the exit. That's when another girl recognized him and pointed him out to others. This must've been when Peter really started to get nervous. Not only had he been recognized twice, but now they were spreading the information. Peter swore with an oath that he didn't know Jesus, ramping up the intensity of his denial. If an oath-taker were lying, the penalty called for divine judgment.

Read Matthew 5:33–37. Summarize Jesus's words below.

Look up Matthew 5:34 in a Greek lexicon. Look up the original word for *oath* and write down what you find.

Look up Matthew 26:72 in a Greek lexicon. Look up the original word for *oath* and write down what you find.

One of the people Peter had been exposed to pushed him a little further, letting him know they didn't believe him. After all, he had the same rural accent as Jesus. Peter and Jesus both lived in Capernaum, a city on the northwest corner of the Sea of Galilee. It was a poor, agrarian community, whereas Jerusalem was a more sophisticated city with a different accent and dialect.

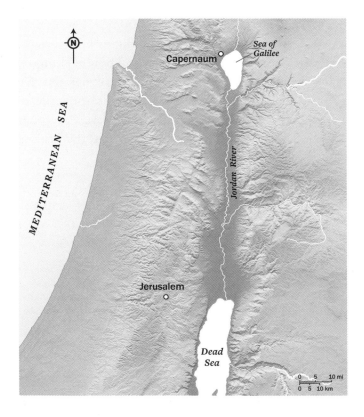

Using a map or a web search, determine the distance between the two cities. Approximately how long would it take to walk from Capernaum to Jerusalem?

Peter once again denied that he knew Jesus, and once again he increased the intensity of his denial—this time using harsh language and invoking a curse on himself.

Look up Matthew 26:74 in a Greek lexicon. Look up the original words for *curse* and *swear* and write down what you find.

After Peter's third denial, just as Jesus prophesied, a rooster crowed. This is significant. God is not just the God of the big details—He's in the small things too. He is sovereign even over the timing of the noises of animals.

Have you ever tried to downplay or hide your relationship with Jesus? How did that feel to you?

Have you ever worried that your sin has disqualified you from being used by God?

The good news for Peter (and for us) is that this isn't the end of his story. God's redemption is always bigger than His kids' rebellion. He's working even our worst acts of sin—which are an affront to the intimate relationship we have with Him—for His glory and our joy (Romans 8:28).

Peter grieved his sin and repented of it. And we'll see how God continued to use him in advancing the gospel. Sinners are all God has to work with, and He delights to give us roles and responsibilities in His kingdom! He's where the joy is!

What stood out to you most in this week's study? Why?

What did you learn or relearn about God and His character this week?

Corresponding Psalm & Prayer

 READ PSALM 55

What correlation do you see between Psalm 55 and this week's study of Jesus and His kingdom?

What portions stand out to you most?

Close by praying this prayer aloud:

Father,
*   I praise You for being sovereign over all the details—big and small. From the timing of Jesus's death lining up with the Passover to the timing of the rooster's crowing, You have Your hands in all things*

and are working them out for Your glory and our joy. Be glorified, God!

You have been merciful to me—You haven't given me the punishment I deserve in response to my sin. And You have been gracious to me—You have given me more than I deserve by adopting me into Your family, giving me the joy of intimacy with You, and equipping me in serving Your kingdom despite my sins and shortcomings!

Father, I have sinned, and I appeal to Your mercy. I repent of my sins and turn to You and ask You to make my heart clean. I confess that, like Peter and Judas, I have chosen my own way over Your ways. I have been greedy, I have lied, and I have sought to protect myself in foolish ways instead of trusting You.

Please fix my eyes on You and Your eternal kingdom, not on the people or things I may be tempted to fear. Please continue to refine me and purify my heart. Reveal the motives of my heart to me. Grant me repentance where I lack it. And grant me continual nearness to You in all things, that I might look more like Your Son, Jesus, as Your Spirit works in me and bears fruit in my life.

I surrender my life to You, Lord—every moment of my day, each decision I make, I yield my will and way to Your perfect will and way.

I love You too. Amen.

Rest, Catch Up, or Dig Deeper

 WEEKLY CHALLENGE

The last line of this week's psalm (Psalm 55) says, "But I will trust in you." The whole psalm is listing out fears and horrors and betrayals of friends—it's heavy with trials and grief. But David wraps it up by basically saying, "Despite all this, I will trust in You." He's reminding his own heart that God is trustworthy despite all the circumstances that may tempt him to doubt God's goodness.

This week your challenge is to begin each day by talking to God about the things that trouble you—either say them out loud or jot them down in your journal as bullet points. There's no need to go into detail for this weekly challenge (and it might even cause you to feel *more* anxious if you do), so be brief if that's helpful. Then, after you've finished telling God about the things that are heavy on your heart, end by saying out loud, "But I will trust in You." You may even want to say this out loud after *each* item.

Remind your heart that God is trustworthy. Remind your heart that after all Jesus endured, God was in the process of redeeming the evil committed against Him. Remind your heart that after all Peter's sin and denial, God's redemption is bigger than his rebellion. Your heart needs regular reminders that God is trustworthy, and it needs a regular call to put that trust into action!

┌ Scripture to Memorize ┐

Therefore do not be anxious about tomorrow, for tomorrow will be anxious for itself. Sufficient for the day is its own trouble.

Matthew 6:34

Matthew 27–28:
Passion of the King

DAILY BIBLE READING

Day 1: Matthew 27:1–26

Day 2: Matthew 27:27–44

Day 3: Matthew 27:45–66

Day 4: Matthew 28:1–10

Day 5: Matthew 28:11–20

Day 6: Psalm 22

Day 7: Catch-Up Day

Corresponds to Days 316 and 318 of *The Bible Recap*.

WEEKLY CHALLENGE

See page 250 for more information.

Matthew 27:1–26

READ MATTHEW 27:1–26

Sometimes, it's easy to breeze past the excruciating torment that our King walked though physically, relationally, mentally, and spiritually on His way to defeating death. This week's study forces our eyes to rest on this painful reality that points us to His ultimate passion—the salvation, redemption, and restoration of all who depend on Him as King.

Review Matthew 26. What things had Jesus already endured?

After an illegal midnight trial, Jesus was found guilty of blasphemy by the religious rulers. However, since they didn't have the power to execute Him, they sent Him to the local Roman governor, Pilate. Pilate had a reputation for being a brutal, corrupt ruler, so the religious leaders expected that getting a death charge from him wouldn't take much arm twisting.

But before Matthew tells us what happened with Pilate, we focus on Judas Iscariot watching the consequences of his choices unfold. In a few short hours, Jesus predicted this relational fracture, then watched it happen—just like with Peter. The offenses—betrayal and denial—are similar, but the two men responded differently to their own sin, yielding a wildly different outcome.

What did Peter's denial of Christ and Judas's betrayal of Christ have in common?

How did they differ?

What are the similarities and differences between the reactions of the two men to their sin?

Look up 27:3 in the following Bible translations and write down the phrase for what Judas did (represented by the Greek word *metamelomai*).

ESV: _____

NIV: _____

CEB: _____

The original language of Scripture reveals a profound difference between feeling personal regret over the consequences of sin (*metamelomai*) and being brokenhearted by the relational fracture sin causes and turning the other direction to walk back toward God in repentance (*metanoeō*, as in Matthew 4:17).

Read 2 Corinthians 7:10. Which kind of grief did Judas have? Which kind of grief did Peter have? How do you know?

When you sin, are you more inclined to feel regret over the consequences of your sin or repentant and brokenhearted over the sin itself?

In Judas's response, the chief priests display their hypocrisy—they're the ones who paid Judas to betray Jesus, but they considered the thirty silver coins "blood money" in the aftermath. Since they couldn't have their "clean" money dirtied, they used the silver to buy a field for burying dead strangers. And with this purchase they accidentally fulfilled Zechariah 11:12–13, reinforcing that the one they would murder is the true King.

When Pilate asked Jesus, "Are you the King of the Jews?", it was likely an ironic or sarcastic question, because the man in front of him had been beaten and bloodied by the Jews and in no way looked the part of a king.

Pilate didn't seem to actually want to put Jesus to death, and even his wife pleaded with him to have nothing to do with bringing Jesus harm in any way. But instead of just releasing Jesus and risking angering the crowds, Pilate tried to use some Jewish religious practices to try to get out of making the call.

Read Leviticus 16:6–10. What happened with the two goats?

Review 27:15–23. What happened with the two men?

What parallels do you see between these two passages?

Believe it or not, Matthew 27 isn't a picture of Leviticus 16—it's the other way around. The practice of slaughtering a goat for a sin offering and letting one go during Passover was a *foretelling* of what Christ would do on this day! In this story, Jesus was the one who became the sin offering, and we're the one who goes free. Jesus was the Savior crucified, and we are Barabbas. We're guilty, deserving of the death penalty, but we go free when the righteous One is slaughtered on our behalf as a sin offering.

Write down a few thoughts or emotions that come to mind when you truly let yourself sit in the fact that *you* are Barabbas in this story.

Pilate was in a tight spot. Meanwhile, the chief priests and elders must have been using some strong manipulation tactics to not only convince the crowd that Jesus should die, but that it should come by crucifixion—a brutal form of Roman execution that the Jews vehemently opposed.

Some today want to use this passage as an excuse for anti-Semitism, but what we see in Genesis 12:3 is that Israel will be both blessed and judged by God. The role of those who follow Christ is to love people in a way that points them to King Jesus and pray for their salvation, not condemn or dismiss them.

Review 27:25. What was the irony of the people suggesting that the blood of Jesus be on them and on their children?

Today's study ends with what might be one of the most redemptively heartbreaking scenes in all of Scripture: The notoriously guilty man is walking free while commands are given to scourge the perfect, innocent King within an inch of His life.

Matthew 27:27–44

◥ **READ MATTHEW 27:27–44**

Having suffered betrayal and beatings, King Jesus was surely sleep-deprived and in anguish. Yet it gets worse before it gets better.

How would you imagine Jesus was feeling in these areas?

Physically: _____

Emotionally: _____

Relationally: _____

Even though Pilate was inclined to release Jesus, it appears that his personal soldiers had their own ideas about what should be done. After Jesus's brutal scourging, they added a stop at the governor's headquarters and invited the whole battalion to join in on the torture.

How is each of these intentional acts of humiliation (from 27:27–29) a direct affront to His position as King? **Use a commentary if it's helpful.**

They stripped Him _____

The scarlet robe _____

The crown of thorns _____

A reed in His right hand _____

Kneeling before Him _____

"Hail, King of the Jews!" _____

The battalion's blatant mocking of Jesus came in the form of ironic cruelty, but we are also guilty of mocking King Jesus any time we live unto ourselves, not submitting to His kingship.

What specific thoughts, actions, or relationships in your life might be mocking Jesus's role as King? Where do you feel a call to submit to His authority?

Jesus was paraded to the site of His execution, Golgotha—the Place of the Skull. But after the pain He endured, He wasn't strong enough to carry the seventy-five pound crossbeam of His execution device. A man named Simon, probably a faithful Jew in town for Passover from more than eight hundred miles away in North Africa, was forced by the Roman soldiers to carry it for Him.

Read 16:24–25. Knowing Jesus was talking about this specific moment, what does it look like to spiritually live out Jesus's call to His disciples?

As was customary, Jesus was offered a drink that could dull His senses, but He refused. Between two common criminals, Jesus's body hung beneath a plaque naming His charges, "This is Jesus, the King of the Jews." The crowd taunted Him to save Himself—and though He was capable of it, He restrained His power and submitted to the Father's plan for our salvation.

Read Hebrews 12:2. What word does the verse use to describe what Jesus was focused on? How does that seem possible in light of all He endured in today's reading?

Matthew 27:45–66

🔻 READ MATTHEW 27:45–66

Though there are no recorded anomalies during the first three hours while Jesus was on the cross (from noon to three in the afternoon), an inexplicable darkness fell over all the earth at the sixth hour as creation mourned the pending death of its Creator. Jesus exclaimed in His native tongue, "My God, my God, why have you forsaken me?"

Many commentaries (and one popular worship song) say this exclamation serves as evidence that God the Father forsook the Son by turning His face away, disconnecting the Son from the Father, presumably because He can't look at sin. However, Scripture never says God cannot look at sin. In fact, throughout the Old Testament God set up camp in the midst of His sinful people and told them to draw *nearer* to Him when they sinned. And Jesus, who *is* God, was near sin all the time but remained sinless.

So what was actually happening when Jesus uttered those words? Here's a helpful theory: It's believed that in ancient times people would reference a given psalm by reciting its first line. Chapter numbers had not yet been assigned to the books of the Bible, and passages were given orally as stories and songs from one generation to the next. So when they wanted to sing a psalm, they couldn't say, "Let's sing Psalm 100" or "Turn to page 523 in your hymnal." They had to rely on the first line to queue up the psalm for the crowd.

When Jesus uttered the first line of Psalm 22, He was likely drawing attention to the whole psalm, which was a prophetic song about the Messiah.

Read Psalm 22. What in this psalm could be prophetic about Jesus? Use a commentary if it's helpful.

Verses 27–28 of the psalm say, "All the ends of the earth shall remember and turn to the LORD, and all the families of the nations shall worship before you. For kingship belongs to the LORD, and he rules over the nations." Our great King Jesus, with His final breaths, declares that His death is to save us. Having undergone a torturous death on the cross, Jesus was thinking about how His death would allow us to be in union with Him forever. It's as if He was crying out, "I'm doing this for you!"

Read John 10:18, 1 John 3:16, Galatians 2:20, and Titus 2:13–14. What do these passages say about Jesus's death?

Review 27:51–54. What miraculous events happened, and what was the spiritual implication of each?

The Miracle	The Implication

How does the centurion respond to the events? How do you think you would've responded?

Because of the Passover holiday, a wealthy follower of Jesus used his status to request his King's body be removed from the cross so that he could give it a proper burial. Jesus was laid in a borrowed tomb, and a large stone was rolled in front of it to seal the opening.

Today's reading concludes with a revealing conversation between religious leaders and Pilate. After clearly stating that Jesus was dead, they recounted Jesus's own words about His resurrection and claimed to want to thwart any attempts to steal His body. But these men had just seen the supernatural events occurring at the death of Jesus and watched His disciples flee into hiding. Their fear isn't likely about the disciples but about the power of Jesus Himself. Pilate gave them an elite guard unit and a governmental seal to secure the tomb. This increased security lends a greater testimony to the power of His pending resurrection.

The religious leaders were trying to use human wisdom, might, and authority to overcome the power of Jesus. While this may seem silly to us, we fall into the same patterns. Unlike those scheming against Jesus, we have access to the power of the resurrected Jesus, and yet often settle for human wisdom, strength, and authority.

Where in your life are you tempted to use human wisdom, strength, or authority when God is offering you His?

Matthew 28:1–10

 READ MATTHEW 28:1-10

Eager to finish the burial preparations that were cut short by the Sabbath, two women arrived outside the tomb before the sun had a chance to break the horizon. Mary Magdalene and "the other Mary" were no doubt filled with grief and still coming to grips with the death of Jesus. Luke's gospel gives us some details about Mary Magdalene—a woman of scandal who was healed by Jesus from seven demons and who sat at the feet of Jesus as a disciple along with the twelve men and two other women (Luke 8:1–3). We don't know many details about who "the other Mary" is, though it may be safe to assume she's the sister of Martha and Lazarus.

What do you think these women were feeling after sitting at the feet of their Rabbi and then watching His death?

Imagine the surprise of these two women and the Roman guards who were guarding the tomb when an angel appeared during a great earthquake to roll away the sealed stone, revealing an empty tomb. The angel had the appearance of lightning (i.e., likely bright or glowing), his clothes were white, he was strong enough to move the stone by himself, and he was apparently tall enough to sit on top of the stone when he finished! However, it's important to note that no one bowed down to worship him.

How did some of Rome's most elite guards respond to the appearance of the angel?

The guards were right to be scared—the resurrection of Jesus should bring terror to the servants of sin. But to the faithful followers of the King, the angel offered comfort. He identified the reason the women came to the tomb, then reset their expectations, letting them know the tomb was empty. This was a paradigm shift for the women, but the angel assured them that it was far better than what they'd imagined.

Why do you think the angel invited the women to look into the tomb with their own eyes?

What are some great things God has done that you've seen with your own eyes?

The angel gave them the directive to tell the disciples Jesus had risen and that He would meet them back in Galilee. And the women wasted no time setting off to complete their mission. Mary and Mary were the first to herald the news of Jesus's resurrection—the first appointed missionaries of what we now call the Church!

Review 28:8. What does it reveal about the emotional state of the women? Do you find this relatable at times when you're called to something for God's glory?

With fear and joy commingled, their quick obedience was rewarded with the unexpected: a visit from the King Himself. With His simple greeting, the women fell to His feet in an emotional moment of worship! Jesus's words reinforced the mission the angel had given them, but Jesus made the message they were to deliver a personal one. The last time the disciples were all together, Jesus told them they'd all fall away, and they did. Yet here, Jesus called them *brothers* for the first time. Their stumbling didn't fracture the affection Jesus had for the men. He had invested three years of His life into His disciples, and despite their downfall, He looked forward to meeting them in Galilee.

What does it reveal about the heart of God that women, who were marginalized in their culture, got the message first?

What are some other times in Matthew's gospel where we've seen Jesus elevate the marginalized above cultural norms?

How does Jesus's continued commitment to an upside-down kingdom encourage your heart? Are there ways it will impact how you live? If so, how?

The King sees and elevates the marginalized, draws near to the lowly, is tender with the brokenhearted, and flips culture on its head when it needs to be set right. He did it in His life, in His death, and once again in His resurrection.

DAY 5

Matthew 28:11–20

◤◢ READ MATTHEW 28:11-20

Matthew's gospel ends with a theme we've seen throughout his account of the life of the King. Some who see and hear the message are unmoved by the evidence of His authority. Others who experience the King find their lives radically transformed, gaining an eternal perspective and a kingdom mission.

Read 1 Corinthians 1:22–25. What two audiences does Paul list? What impact does the cross have on each audience?

In this final chapter of Matthew, Mary and Mary took the message of the resurrection to the disciples while the guards made their way into the city to tell the chief priests their unfortunate news. At that point, the religious leaders could no longer deny that Jesus was the King—but instead of bending the knee, they schemed to cover it up. This scenario reveals what Jesus had been saying all along: It's possible to know the truth and be unmoved by it.

In your own words, describe the cover-up plan. How was this plan problematic?

Between the silver they paid to Judas (roughly four months' wages) and the "sufficient sum" paid to the guards, the chief priests spent a lot of money on the plot to kill Jesus—to no avail. Another problem is that the guards also had to agree to the unlikely scenario in which they were all asleep at the same time, no one was awakened by the noise or the earthquake, and they knew for sure that the disciples stole the body. A basic understanding of the facts could override any defenses they might have presented.

Why do you think the chief priests doubled down instead of admitting they were wrong?

Do you ever find yourself too stubborn to admit you're wrong when God is showing you something that needs to change in your life? How do you respond?

Jesus met His disciples in the Galilee region, just as He promised. We know from other gospel accounts that this wasn't their first meeting with the resurrected Jesus, but it was an important one. As is common with an encounter with the resurrected King, they all worshiped immediately, but according to Matthew, some still doubted. The original word for *doubt* here points to an uncertainty and hesitation, not a settled disbelief. These men had their world shaken up, and it's understandable that some of them had a hard time taking in all the facts at play.

Describe a time when you experienced or learned something that led to a paradigm shift. What did this growth process feel like? How long did it take you to process the new information?

During their time together—even in their doubt—Jesus commissioned them to spread the good news of His resurrection.

Review 28:18–20. What was included in Jesus's instructions, and what was His promise? How might His promise have given the disciples hope for such a large task?

Jesus, claiming the authority of God (because He *is* God), commanded them to go and to make disciples. He wasn't talking about converts, neutral supporters, or churchgoers whose attendance does little to inform their lives. *Disciple* means "learner." This was a call to continually teach others about the things they'd learned from the King.

Read Genesis 17:10–11. What was the physical sign of the covenant between God and Israel? What was the sign given to the disciples for the new covenant?

What is the significance of being baptized in the name of the Father, Son, and Holy Spirit? What role does each of them play in the salvation of Christ-followers?

If the Trinity is a relatively unknown concept to you, dig a little deeper! The more we come to know God in each of His persons, the more we can be like Him in fulfilling this international task of disciple making!

Review 28:20b. Does the promise Jesus made apply to believers today? What kind of comfort does this give you as you consider the call to make disciples?

While we all have the call to make disciples, our primary motive shouldn't be one of obligation but one of delight! We deserve death, yet our King Jesus experienced the worst death known to mankind so that we could glorify Him with our lives and spend eternity with Him. This message that starts with our depravity ends with an eternal hope and an upside-down kingdom. In His kingdom, the least are elevated, the last are first, the sick are made well, and the Savior of our souls knows and loves us fully. Our hearts long for that eternal kingdom with our King, because He's where the joy is!

What stood out to you most in this week's study? Why?

What did you learn or relearn about God and His character this week?

Corresponding Psalm & Prayer

 READ PSALM 22

What correlation do you see between Psalm 22 and this week's study of Jesus and His kingdom?

What portions stand out to you most?

Close by praying this prayer aloud:

Father,
*   I praise You for Your perfect plan for our redemption. Even before You created the world, You had a plan in place to bring us into Your eternal kingdom. You are so generous—abundantly gracious and*

audaciously merciful. Father, thank You for adopting us into Your family. Jesus, thank You for living a righteous life and granting us that righteousness, then taking our sin in exchange and receiving the penalty we deserve. Spirit, thank You for dwelling in us and marking us as members of the kingdom!

Father, I have sinned, and I appeal to Your mercy. I confess that I easily disregard the weight of Your Son's sacrifice—I exchange the freedom of obedience for the bondage of my chosen sins. Like the disciples, I've had moments of doubt, yet You have always welcomed and loved me regardless. I repent of my sins and turn to You and ask You to make my heart clean.

After all I've learned about You, help me to do more than just keep these beautiful truths to myself. Prompt me to make disciples—to teach others what I've learned. Create divine opportunities, soften hearts, and give me the words to say as I invite others to join Your kingdom or to know more about the King Himself!

I surrender my life to You, Lord—every moment of my day, each decision I make, I yield my will and way to Your perfect will and way.

I love You too. Amen.

Rest, Catch Up, or Dig Deeper

 WEEKLY CHALLENGE

Read 1 Timothy 6:11–16. Paul wrote this letter to his young protégé to remind him to keep fighting the good fight of faith. In this passage, he recounts the events of Matthew 27–28 and points our hope toward the kingship of Christ!

Having studied how Matthew reveals Jesus as King, write a few paragraphs in your journal using these three prompts:

1. How does the kingship of Jesus inform the way I live my life every day? (If it doesn't, spend some time here journaling out a prayer. Ask God to move your heart toward action based on what you've been studying for the past ten weeks.)

2. If a Christian friend asked me if it really mattered that Jesus is King, I would tell them . . .

3. If a friend who doesn't know Jesus asked why we call Him "King Jesus," I would tell them . . .

FOR GROUP LEADERS

Thank you for using this study and leading others through it as well! Each week has a wide variety of content (content and questions, daily Bible reading, Scripture memorization, weekly challenge, and resources) to help the reader develop a range of spiritual disciplines. Feel free to include as much or as little of that in your meetings as you'd like. The details provided in How to Use This Study (pp. 13–14) will be helpful to you and all your group members, so be sure to review that information together!

It's up to you and your group how you'd like to structure your meetings, but we suggest including time for discussion of the week's study and Bible text, mutual encouragement, and prayer. You may also want to practice your Scripture memory verses together as a group or in pairs. As you share with each other, "consider how to stir up one another to love and good works" (Hebrews 10:24) and "encourage one another and build one another up" (1 Thessalonians 5:11).

Here are some sample questions to help facilitate discussion. This is structured as a weekly study, but if your group meets at a different frequency, you may wish to adjust the questions accordingly. Cover as many questions as time allows, or feel free to come up with your own. And don't forget to check out the additional resources we've linked for you at MyDGroup.org/Resources/Matthew.

Sample Discussion Questions

What questions did this week's study or Bible text bring up for you?

What stood out to you in this week's study?

What did you notice about God and His character?

How were you challenged by your study of the Bible text? Is there anything you want to change in light of what you learned?

How does what you learned about God affect the way you live in community?

What correlation did you see between the psalm from Day 6 and this week's study of Jesus and His kingdom?

Have you felt God working in you through the weekly challenge? If so, how?

Is your love for God's Word increasing as we go through this study? If so, how?

Did anything you learned increase your joy in knowing Jesus?

ACKNOWLEDGMENTS

It was my great joy to be just one among a team of writers on this project. Laura Buchelt, Emily Pickell, Evaline Asmah, and Meg Mitchell—thank you for your incredible research, creativity, wisdom, humility, and laughter. I never knew an ironing board could serve as a writing desk or that a raccoon Snuggie would be the perfect outfit to stimulate creativity. And to LB especially—thank you for all your prep work to divide this study into segments and to fight writer's block by mandating a cold plunge.

Olivia Le handled all the practical details for our writing retreat—from booking flights to feeding us to helping us find the best hike when we needed a brief respite from our laptops. She also makes the best scrambled eggs on God's green earth.

Without the ongoing wisdom and encouragement from Lisa Jackson, my literary agent, none of this would be possible. And to her husband, Rich, who surely delivered no fewer than fifty boxes of materials for us, plus a card table.

My editors, Jeff Braun and Hannah Ahlfield, are truly the dream team for me. Thank you for sharing this vision to help people unearth more layers of the beauty of God's Word. Here's to many more celebratory energy drinks!

And to the rest of the incredible D-Group Team—Rachel Mantooth, Lindsay Ruhter, Warwick Fuller, and Omar Cardenas—our board, and all our leaders and members around the world. I love being on mission with you!

ABOUT THE EDITOR

TARA-LEIGH COBBLE'S zeal for biblical literacy led her to create a network of Bible studies called D-Group (Discipleship Group). Every week, hundreds of men's and women's D-Groups meet in homes, in churches, and online for Bible study and accountability.

She also writes and hosts a daily podcast called *The Bible Recap* designed to help listeners read and understand the Bible in a year. The podcast garnered over three hundred million downloads in its first five years, and more than twenty thousand churches around the world have joined their reading plan to know and love God better. It has been turned into a book published by Bethany House Publishers.

Tara-Leigh is a *Wall Street Journal* bestselling author, speaks to a wide variety of audiences, and regularly leads teaching trips to Israel because she loves to watch others be awed by the story of Scripture through firsthand experience.

Her favorite things include sparkling water and days that are 72 degrees with 55 percent humidity, and she thinks every meal tastes better when eaten outside. She lives in a concrete box in the skies of Dallas, Texas, where she has no pets, children, or anything that might die if she forgets to feed it.

For more information about Tara-Leigh and her ministries, you can visit her online.

Websites: taraleighcobble.com | thebiblerecap.com | mydgroup.org | israelux.com
Social media: @taraleighcobble | @thebiblerecap | @mydgroup | @israeluxtours